HIDDEN HISTORY

of the

NEW HAMPSHIRE SEACOAST

HIDDEN HISTORY *of the* NEW HAMPSHIRE SEACOAST

Terry Nelson

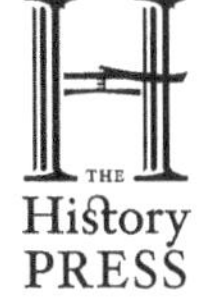

Published by The History Press
Charleston, SC
www.historypress.com

First published 2019

Manufactured in the United States

ISBN 9781467143394

Library of Congress Control Number: 2019936991

Notice: The information in this book is true and complete to the best of our knowledge. It is offered without guarantee on the part of the author or The History Press. The author and The History Press disclaim all liability in connection with the use of this book.

For my wife, Barbara—
without her this wouldn't have happened.
And to our sons, Chris and Jeff, and their families—
the lights of our lives.

Contents

Preface

When my wife, Barbara, and I moved to Dover, New Hampshire, from Michigan, one of the first things we did was drive around exploring our new home state. Often, when we drove through a wooded area, whether on the freeway or down two-lanes, we would see stone walls off to the side and say to each other, "What are all these walls doing in the middle of the woods?!" (Also, driving through Dover on our first October 30, we wondered, "Why are all these kids walking around town in costumes on the night before Halloween?" but that's a story for another time.) Those mysterious walls and many subsequent similar experiences made me realize that, aside from the numerous important and well-known historical places in our state, New Hampshire is filled with many others that are hidden away but well worth exploring if one knows the story behind them.

My first job in New Hampshire was working as a special education consultant for Granite State College (which certainly made it easy for me to remember the state nickname). I was assigned to work with sixteen school districts in the south central part of the state. As such, I had to do a lot of driving around from my home on the seacoast to the various schools in that region. Since many of them were in rural areas and small towns, I had the opportunity to start running across many hidden or out-of-the-way sites. The stories behind these places range from a small, easy-to-miss marker commemorating a country doctor turned military leader joining one of the most famous battles in American history (everyone driving a Ford knows his name—and it's not Ford!), to a "pile of rocks" that held up a $44 million high school project, to a bear cage restored by an Eagle Scout at New Hampshire's own Central Park and on to a monument looking out toward the Great Bay dedicated to a selfless young man by his grieving friends from Salem, Massachusetts.

In this book, I have compiled the stories of ten widely varied and pretty much little-known historic spots from all around New Hampshire's seacoast. I have taken the liberty to broaden the definition of the seacoast a bit to encompass all of Rockingham and Strafford Counties, both of which access the sea. Along the way, I have learned of many fascinating people and little-known events that have transpired in our state that I hope to bring to light, not the least of which is how much we owe to the Daughters of the American Revolution and Boy Scouts for faithfully identifying and preserving our past.

I hope you enjoy my journey as we explore these special places and stories that deserve not to be forgotten.

Acknowledgements

With stories as varied as these, I had to do a lot of traveling and visiting to get information, materials and images. Along the way, I had the pleasure of meeting dozens of new people without whom there would have been no way I could have written this book. And, of course, I also got tremendous assistance with many people whom I already did know. I'd like to thank them all now.

My brother, Dr. Tim Nelson, DVM, of Port St. Joe, Florida, is an ace with photography to whom I sent dozens of photos to polish up for me. Frank Kennedy, a curator at the Summersworth Historical Society and Museum, has been an invaluable help in providing photos, materials and local contacts. He has a wealth of knowledge about Dover Speedway and Central Park. My friends and former Southside Middle School colleagues Elizabeth Ellis and Don Menswar were very helpful in giving my early manuscripts a read and suggesting some very useful and needed improvements. Carol Pynn from the Windham Historical Commission provided some great insight into the effort to save the London Bridge Causeway. My appreciation also goes to Mike Day, operations manager at the Woodman Museum in Dover, for allowing me to photograph some of the museum's treasures, as well as providing research assistance. Historian, author and St. Anselm College professor Robert Perreault was most helpful in guiding me through the publishing process. A very big thanks to the staff at the excellent Dover Public Library for all their help guiding me toward obscure books, subjects and unique materials. The history room there is incredible. Last, but certainly not least, thanks to Dr. Mary Ford for hiring me as a special education consultant at Granite State College, thereby allowing me to wander the state while doing my job.

My thanks and appreciation also go out to all those who helped with individual chapters:

Dr. Dearborn: Katherine Fernald, Else Cilley Chapter, Daughters of the American Revolution; Nottingham Historical Society–Van Dame Museum; Portsmouth Athenaeum; New Hampshire Historical Society.

London Bridge: Tanya Krajcik, New Hampshire Division of Historical Resources; Windham Historical Commission; Nick Letizio.

Little Boar's Head: Hampton Historical Society, Tuck Museum; USS Albacore Museum, Portsmouth; Lane Memorial Library, Hampton; North Hampton Public Library.

The Meeting House at Dover Point: Diane Fisk, First Parish Church, Dover; Alena Warren, Strafford County Conservation District.

Broth Hill: Nancy Sandberg, Durham Historic Association.

Town Pounds: Daniel Peters, Jeffery Barraclough, John Clayton, Manchester Historical Association; Matthew Thomas, Fremont Historical Association.

Dover Speedway: Tanya Krajcik, NHDHR; Alena Warren, SCCD; Charlie Crocco Jr.; New Hampshire Historical Society.

Atkinson Academy: Adele Dillon, Atkinson Historical Society; Kimball Library, Atkinson; New Hampshire Historical Society.

Central Park: David Brackett; Mike Gillis.

John Leighton: Betsey Bennett, Tabernacle Church of Salem, Massachusetts; Nancy Leighton Auclair; Gayle Van Dyke; Portsmouth Athenaeum; Diane Fiske.

Finally, I'd like to acknowledge my mother, whose love of history inspired that same love in me; and my father, who, in inviting me to ride along on business trips to various states, started me on the path to my love of exploring new places and things.

Dr. Dearborn, the DAR and Nottingham Square

I eat part of a fryed Rattle Snake to day, which would have tasted very well had it not been snake.
—Henry Dearborn

On April 19, 1775, after Paul Revere, William Dawes and James Prescott gave their famous warnings, Massachusetts Minutemen engaged British Regulars at Lexington and Concord in what came to be known forever after as "the shot heard round the world." The next morning, the "Concord Alarm" reached New Hampshire. Before long, hundreds of New Hampshiremen were headed across the Merrimack. "We go to the assistance of our brethren" was their call to action. By two o'clock, over sixty men with muskets and equipment had met up with local militia leaders Henry Dearborn and Joseph Cilley Jr. at the meetinghouse on Nottingham Square, ready to march. Among those joining them were Amos Morrill, Michael McClary (nephew of Andrew McClary, for whom Fort McClary in Kittery, Maine, is named), Neal and Andrew McGuffey, Weymouth Wallace, Bennet Libby and William McCrillis, all from Epson; Joseph Jackson, Robert Morrison and John Nealley from Nottingham; Andrew Neally from Deerfield; and Jonathan Clarke from Northwood.

The company set off for the assigned militia mustering camp at Cambridge, Massachusetts. Running rather than marching, they covered the twenty-seven miles to the ferry at Haverhill by dusk. After the ferry crossing, they stopped in Andover to eat and then continued on to the Cambridge parade ground, covering the final twenty-eight miles by sunrise of the twenty-first. The entire fifty-five-mile journey took less than twenty hours. Do the math! These rugged Patriots averaged nearly three miles an hour, mostly at night, on foot, fully equipped for battle and taking time out to get across the Merrimack River and have supper.

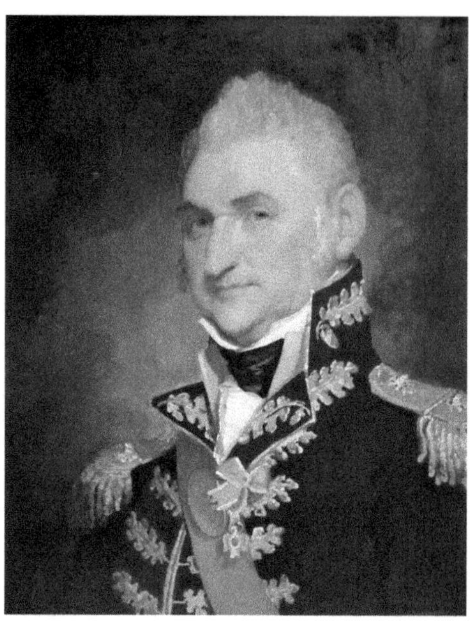

General Henry Dearborn by Gilbert Stuart, 1812. *Courtesy of the Art Institute of Chicago.*

Nottingham Square is a hidden gem. It has a beautiful, unspoiled green bordered on the west by NH Route 156. It is just up the road from the entrance to Pawtuckaway Park, and it is bisected by Farm Ledge Road, the old road to Epping. It is surrounded by farms still worked by descendants of the men who made that incredible march as well as the earliest settlers. Being situated on a large, flat hilltop, from the square you can see nearly to the seacoast in the winter when the leaves are down.

Nottingham is known as the town of four generals. Passing through the square, which at one time was the parade ground for militias, you can't miss the impressive Minuteman statue with the names of Revolutionary War generals Thomas Bartlett (whose sister Mary was married to Henry Dearborn), Henry Butler, Joseph Cilley Jr. and Henry Dearborn emblazoned around its base. This statue, dedicated on July 4, 1917, is among many other historical monuments commemorating places or events, from old tavern sites to Native American skirmishes to the last slave in our state. They have been placed around Nottingham by the Else Cilley Chapter of the Daughters of the American Revolution. One of those monuments, tucked away on the east side of Route 156 and just north of the square, commemorates the militia's remarkable achievement. Up until this day, many of the regents of the Else Cilley DAR chapter are Cilley descendants. There is a Cilley Road in Manchester, and a Cilley has until recently served as a member of the New Hampshire House of Representatives and Senate. In older times, there have been Cilleys in the U.S. Senate, the New Hampshire

State Senate and another in the New Hampshire House. For good measure, there is a Cilley State Forest in Concord. I think it's safe to say they have had a rather large impact on our state.

As the New Hampshire Minutemen, now numbering over two thousand, were converging within three miles of Cambridge, they were met by a man representing himself as an officer. He announced that their services were not needed and that they had been dismissed by General Artemus Ward. As word of this spread, hundreds of militia men turned around and headed back home. When their commanders found out that this was a hoax, they sent messengers to try to get the men to come back, but many had gone too far by then to be reached. A few weeks later, on May 15, the Nottingham town council voted to pay the Minutemen three shillings a day (about twenty-five dollars today) for their service but with the proviso that nothing was to be paid to those who went home early—not even for their twenty-hour march!

One of the commanders, Andrew McClary, was so concerned about how this perceived incident of desertion might reflect badly on the New Hampshire soldiers that he wrote a letter to the Provincial Congress asking for its understanding. Part of his explanation included the exchange with the mysterious officer: "Yesterday it was reported throughout the New Hampshire Troops that one Mr. Esquire [meaning a person not known to them, "esquire" being a general term for a gentleman] who appeared in the character of a Capt. at the Head of a Company, had been to the general and had received a verbal express from him that all New Hampshire Troops were dismissed and that they might return home." After McClary signed the letter, he added a postscript: "Take notice, I never told you that Squire Samuel Dudley was the man who propagated this groundless report." (Modern translation: "I'm spilling the beans on Samuel Dudley as 'Mr. Esquire,' but you didn't hear it from me!")

Although the New Hampshire men were too late for the Battles of Lexington and Concord, on April 23, Colonel John "Live free or die: Death is not the worst of evils" Stark organized the First New Hampshire Regiment. At age twenty-four, Henry Dearborn was made a captain of a company—by far the youngest officer in the regiment. Less than two months later, with Stark's unit now encamped at Medford, Massachusetts, the New Hampshire Minutemen were to join in at the Battle of Bunker Hill. In 1818, Henry Dearborn published *An Account of the Battle of Bunker Hill*. Genera Dearborn's diary best describes some of the events of that pivotal day, June 17, 1775:

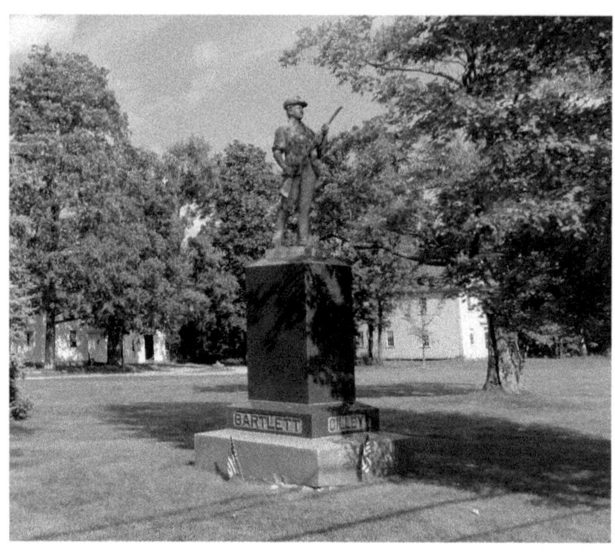

The four generals Minuteman statue at Nottingham Square with the Old School House behind and to the right. *Author's photo.*

> *The regiment, being destitute of ammunition, formed in front of a house occupied as an arsenal, where each man was given a gill cup full of powder, fifteen balls and one flint....As there were scarcely two muskets in a company of equal calibre, it was necessary to reduce the size of the balls for many of them....*
>
> *After completing the necessary preparations for action, the regiment formed and marched about one o'clock.... When we reached Bunker Hill... the regiment halted for a few minutes for the rear to come up. Soon after, the enemy were discovered to have landed on the shore at Morten's Point, in front of Breed's Hill, undercover of a tremendous fire of shot and shell, from a battery on Copp's Hill....*
>
> *The veteran and gallant Stark harangued his regiment in a short but animated address, then directed them to give three cheers, and made a rapid movement to the rail fence which ran from the left...toward the Mystic River.*
>
> *The action soon became general, and very heavy from left to right. In ten or fifteen minutes the enemy gave way at all points, and retreated in great disorder.*

In the 1939 publication *The Revolutionary War Journals of Henry Dearborn*, biographer Henry Dunlap Smith sums up Dearborn's leadership, bravery and humility perfectly in the following paragraph:

> *General Howe's veteran British regulars attempted three times to storm the hill, which was held by a motley handful of undisciplined volunteers*

barricaded behind a hastily constructed redoubt and a post-and-rail fence. Among the defenders of the fence was Captain Dearborn, who was on Colonel Stark's right wing. Of these men, Dearborn later said, "Not an officer or soldier of the continental troops engaged was in uniform but were in the plain and ordinary dress of citizens; nor was there an officer on horseback." Only when their ammunition was exhausted did the American troops retreat towards Bunker Hill. The significance of the battle lies largely in the stubborn resistance of the provincials, who, by driving the British regulars back in disorder two times, showed the colonies that there was hope of ultimate victory in their struggle for independence.

The Else Cilley Chapter of the Nottingham DAR, founded in 1898, is named after Alice "Else" (pronounced "Elsie") Rawlins, wife of Captain Joseph Cilley and mother of General Joseph Cilley Jr., the latter of whom is one of the four generals on the Minuteman statue. The decision to name this particular DAR chapter after Else was an easy one, as all of the twelve founding members were directly descended from her. One of those descendants, Laura A. Marston (also a descendent of Henry's mother, Sarah Marston), was the chapter regent responsible for installing the Dearborn monument in 1905. The small stone block nestled in some bushes is very easy to miss, being only about eighteen inches high and roughly the same width. It reads:

GEN. HENRY DEARBORN
1751 __ 1829
MARCHED WITH 60
MINUTE MEN FROM
NOTTINGHAM SQUARE
TO BUNKER HILL
IN 12 HOURS
APRIL 20, 1775
ERECTED BY DAR
AUG. 1905

Now, careful readers may have noticed a couple of discrepancies here. Most histories relate that the march took something under twenty hours. The Minutemen would have to have been hot-footing it indeed to go fifty-five miles in twelve hours, including time out to get sixty men across the Merrimack by ferry and then stopping to eat. And the author of the tablet

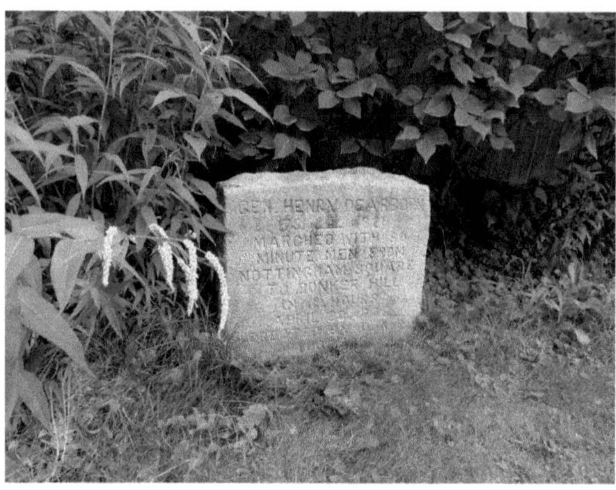

The Dearborn Monument just north of Nottingham Square. *Author's photo.*

seemed to have made the decision to conflate the actual march destination of Cambridge with the company's appearance at the Battle of Bunker Hill almost two months later. Given all that, however, those discrepancies don't matter much at all due to the simple fact that this little stone brings to life a lot of history—and it certainly does not diminish the amazing feat that these young Patriots accomplished.

There are several other DAR monuments scattered around the square and nearby, but another fascinating attraction is the old schoolhouse, visible from NH 156, which is owned by the Else Cilley DAR. It was built in 1850 on the site of a 1770 schoolhouse, and the DAR holds its meetings on the first floor, while the second floor has been turned into an outstanding museum of the school's history (originally the classroom was on the first floor and a community center on the second) run by the Nottingham Historical Society. It may be visited by appointment. It includes rows of original student desks, several made by local townsfolk. There are many other artifacts as well, including a very rare forty-six-star American flag (bonus points if you can name that forty-sixth state; answer at the end of the paragraph) and, most amazing, some wall graffiti referencing Bible verses from the books of Isaiah and Matthew in an anteroom, dated 1852 and 1854, and with what appears to be the name "Mr. Littlefield" underneath. Checking out these two verses as best as possible reveals that they both seemed to deal with lots of biblical misbehavior, the Lord's vengeance and redemption. It's probably quite safe to assume that there were some naughty doings being dealt with. The mystery is whether Mr. Littlefield was the detention-assigning headmaster or one of the young miscreants. Either way, the museum is so authentic that you can almost feel as if you were back there with those boys in the 1850s, especially as you look out the windows and see that the view outside, including the parade ground where Dearborn trained his militia, has changed little since those days.

(Answer: Oklahoma, admitted 1907, which means that flag was current for just five years.)

Henry Dearborn was born in North Hampton on February 23, 1751. He was the twelfth child in his family, and his father was the ninth in his (one of his uncles had seventeen children; frankly, given that productivity, it's a bit surprising that there aren't a lot more Dearborns running around New

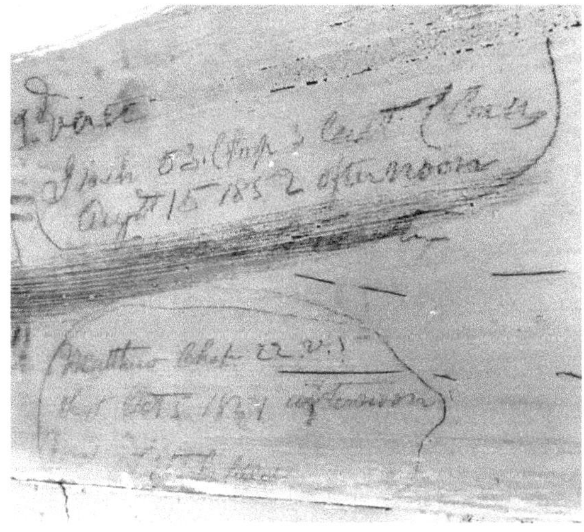

Nottingham old schoolhouse graffiti. *Author's photo with permission of the Else Cilley DAR.*

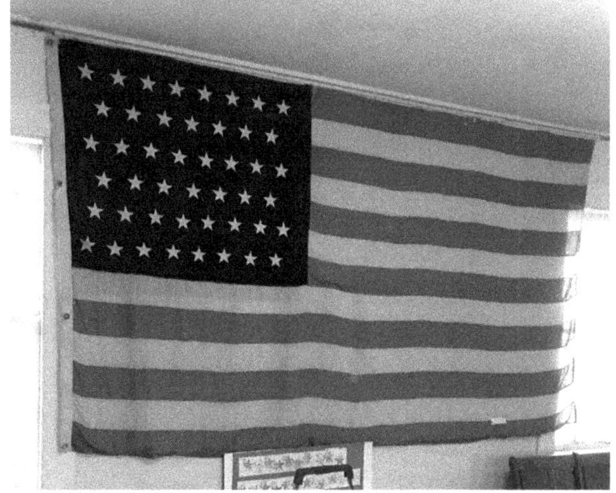

The forty-six-star flag at the old schoolhouse, Nottingham Square. *Author's photo with permission of the Else Cilley DAR.*

Hampshire). Henry spent much of his youth in Epping, where, according to biographer Henry Dunlap Smith, he was a strong, athletic boy and a champion wrestler. In 1771, he married Mary Bartlett, and they had two daughters, Sophia and Pamela Augusta. Henry took his medical instruction from Dr. Hall Jackson of Portsmouth (himself a distinguished surgeon in the army during the Revolution) and in 1772 set up his medical practice in Nottingham, just off the square. His DAR monument is placed at the site of his home, which is no longer standing. He quickly earned high esteem in Nottingham, not only as a physician but also by serving as town auditor and moderator. Most significantly (as told by biographer Charles Coffin), at the age of twenty-one, three years before the war, Henry Dearborn "with several gentlemen of the neighborhood...employed his leisure hours in military exercises; being convinced that the time was rapidly approaching when the liberties of this country must be either shamefully surrendered or boldly defended."

Dearborn's heroics at Bunker Hill were only the beginning of his Revolutionary War service. His interactions and appearances with famous persons read like a Hollywood movie. In addition to Colonel Stark, he served under Benedict Arnold, befriended Aaron Burr, was with General Washington at Valley Forge and then later on was at Yorktown for Lord Cornwallis's surrender to end the war. Dearborn played an integral role at the successful Battles of Saratoga, where one of the British prisoners taken was John Whistler, grandfather of artist James McNeill Whistler. Whistler later changed teams and joined the American army.

Perhaps Dearborn's greatest war travail was his march to Quebec to join Colonel Benedict Arnold in the effort to take Montreal and Quebec City. Leaving his encampment at Winter Hill in Somerville, Massachusetts, on September 10, 1775 (less than two months after Bunker Hill—without any pay for him or his men since June 1), Dearborn's company sailed to Fort Western, in what is now Augusta, Maine, arriving on September 27. From there, the plan was to follow the Kennebec River north to the Chaudière River in Quebec—more than three hundred miles through the wilderness. Dearborn and several of his company used *bateaux*, a type of flat-bottomed boat, on the river, with the rest of the men marching on land alongside. Probably the best day-to-day accounting of the war anywhere are Dearborn's Revolutionary War journals. Covering the period from 1775 to 1783, they describe battles, strategies, hardships, celebrations and even his own personal heartbreaks, all in real time. His journals make up six volumes, but a few select quotes can give a feeling for what it was like to live through that experience (bear in mind that there was no common spelling at that time):

Oct. 17 [1775]—*We proceeded up the river ten miles and came to an Indian Wig-Wam, said to belong to an old Indian called Nattannas. It stands on a point of land beautifully situated, there is a number of acres of clear'd land about it...*[Nattannas, a Norridgewock Native American, was initially thought to be a British spy but turned out to be a friend and guide. He fought side by side with the Americans and was wounded at Quebec.]

Oct. 18—The weather is very rainy to day....I had a quarter of beef served to my Company....

Oct. 19—The weather rainy....We set off from this place proceeded up the river five miles, pass'd several small falls and then encamped.

Oct. 20—Proceeded up the river, pass'd by several small falls, one carrying place....The weather rainy all day we suppose this march to be 13 miles.

Oct. 21—We proceeded up the river 3 miles to a carrying place, carry'd across and continued our route up the river....It rained very fast all night, the river rose fast.

Oct. 22—The river has risen eight or nine feet, which renders it very bad getting up....Our whole march to day is not more than four miles, the river rising so much, fills the low ground so full of water, that our men on shore have found it very difficult and tedious marching.

Oct. 23—We continued our march, tho. very slow by reason of the rapidity of the stream, a very unlucky accident happen'd to us to-day, the most of our men by land miss'd their way and marched their way up a small river....We fancied they took a wrong course, I sent my batteau up that four miles...found the foot people had cross'd the river on a tree and had struck a course for the Dead River....We found our foot-men at the foot of these falls, several batteaus overset [overturned], *which were entirely lost...a considerable quantity of cloathing, guns and provisions...sent back 26 sick men under the command....*

Oct. 25—This night I was seized with a violent head-ache and fever, Charles gather'd me some herbs in the woods and made me tea of them, I drank very hearty of it and next morning felt much better.

Oct. 28—...Cap. Goodrich was almost perished with the cold, having waded several miles backwards and forwards, sometimes to his arm-pits in water & ice, endeavouring to find some place to cross this river....

Oct. 31—We started very early this morning, I am still more unwell than I was yesterday.

Dearborn's long, dreadful march was completed in early November. Upon arrival at the Chaudière, he came down with a severe fever, such that he could not go on for ten days. His company went on toward Quebec City without him and joined with the rest of Arnold's army to prepare for the assault on Quebec. Once he recovered his health, Dearborn traveled to meet up with his company and, on December 31, was given orders to attack. As a snowstorm raged, Dearborn's company advanced to what turned out to be overwhelming British numbers. He was forced to surrender, and he and his men were taken prisoner. Henry was held for several months until he was exchanged for the family of Tory Peter Livius, formerly of New Hampshire and now living in Quebec, whose wife and children were being held in Portsmouth.

Despite all the fighting and hardships, however, there were some opportunities for a bit of R&R. Jumping ahead a few years, with a few toast samples celebrating American independence:

> *July 5* [1779]—*Gen. Poor made an entertainment to day for all officers of his Brigade, to celebrate the Anniversary of the declaration of American Independence. 87 Gentlemen were at dinner, after which the 13 following Patriotick toasts were drank....*
> *1st.* [toast]—*4th of July 76, the ever memoriable Era of American Independence*
> *2d.—the United States*
> *4th—Gen. Washington & the Army*
> *5th—the King & Queen of France*
> *8th—May the counsellors of America be wise, and her Soldiers Invincible.*
> *11th—the Immortal memory of those heroes that have fallen in defense of Liberty*
> *12th—May this New World be the last Asylum for freedom and the arts.*

But then, just two days later, back to reality:

> *July 7—I eat part of a fryed Rattle Snake to day, which would have tasted very well had it not been snake.*

In the midst of his war service (and going back a year), Dearborn's journal also recorded a great personal tragedy: the death of his wife of seven years, Mary Bartlett, at the age of twenty-seven. He arrived home just hours before she died:

> *Oct. 19* [1778]—*We march at 10 O Clock towards Hartford. I receiv'd news this day by express that my wife lay dangerously sick with a nervous*

> *fever. In consequence of which I got leave of absence & set out for home this evening.*
> *Oct. 24—I arrived at my house* [in Nottingham] *at 7 O Clock in the evening. Found my wife senceless & almost motionless, which was a very shocking sight to behold, at half after eleven she expired, much lamented not only by her relation but by all her neighbours....I seem to be quite alone in the world. Except but my two little daughters who are too small to feel their loss....*
> *Oct. 25—The most malloncolly* [sic] *Sunday I ever experienced.*

Mary was laid to rest on October 26, and by November 1, Henry was back in camp. By now, Dearborn had advanced to the rank of lieutenant colonel. Earlier that year, he had distinguished himself and his regiment with a courageous charge at the Battle of Monmouth, for which General Washington awarded him a commendation. By the time he arrived at Yorktown for Cornwallis's surrender in 1781, he had been made deputy quartermaster general of the army and then was commissioned as a full colonel of the First New Hampshire Regiment. The previous year, he married Dorcas Marble, with whom he had two more children. He retired from the army in 1783, and in 1784, he and his new wife moved to Pittsdown, Maine, a place that had impressed him with its beauty when he passed through in 1775 on the way to his long march to Quebec. It was in Maine that his second career as a politician began when, in 1787, Washington designated him as the first United States marshal for the District of Maine. In that same year, the State of Massachusetts appointed him a major general of the Maine militia (Maine was part of Massachusetts until 1820). He was elected to the U.S. House of Representatives in 1792, serving for two terms. In 1801, newly elected president Thomas Jefferson appointed Dearborn to his cabinet as secretary of war. Later, Dearborn served as a major general in the War of 1812.

Although Henry Dearborn is a historical star in Nottingham, interviews with several townsfolk revealed that very few of them connected his name to that of Dearborn, Michigan. To anyone living in Michigan, the suburban Detroit city of Dearborn is as familiar as Manchester is to anyone from New Hampshire. The Ford Motor Company World Headquarters is there. It might as well be a state law that every school for one hundred miles around take its kids on frequent field trips to the Henry Ford Museum and Greenfield Village in Dearborn. Among the thousands of artifacts of American life and industry in the half-million-square-foot museum—ranging from planes to

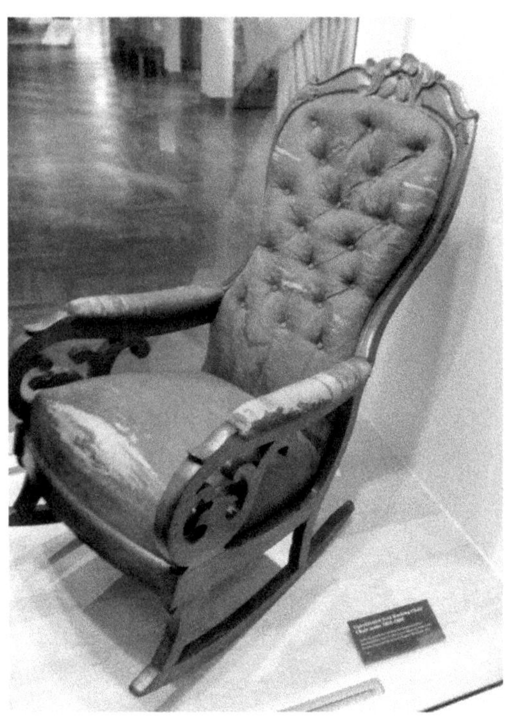

Lincoln's chair from Ford's Theatre, now in Dearborn, Michigan. *Courtesy of tomabouttown.wordpress.com.*

locomotives and, of course, cars—is a letter purported to be from Bonnie Parker's friend Clyde Barrow to Henry Ford extolling the virtues of the Ford V8 as a getaway car. A large concrete square signed by Henry Ford's good friend Thomas Edison in honor of the museum's opening in 1929 is proudly displayed in the lobby. Abraham Lincoln's fateful seat from Ford's Theatre, the presidential limousine John F. Kennedy rode in on his last ride and Rosa Parks's bus are all there.

The city of Dearborn, Michigan, began as an arsenal called Dearbornville, so named by Lieutenant Joshua Howard in honor of General Henry Dearborn, under whom he served during the War of 1812. Lieutenant Howard had been commissioned by the U.S. Army to build the arsenal to serve Detroit, just a few miles to the east, in 1833. Although the city of Dearborn is known throughout the world, it was another Henry who made it famous when he moved his Ford Motor Company's headquarters there in 1928.

Just as every Michigander (or is it Michiganian? it depends on which of the two Detroit newspapers one reads) knows of the town of Dearborn, likewise every Chicagoan knows Dearborn Street, which runs north and south through the heart of the city. In 1795, at the conclusion of the

Northwest Indian War, the Treaty of Greenville (Ohio) was concluded between U.S. General "Mad" Anthony Wayne and several allied Native American nations, including the Wyandot, Miami and Chippewa. This agreement ceded to the United States a large tract of land in Ohio, as well as several "isolated reservations" (as told by Chicago historian Milo Quaife), including "one piece of land six miles square at the mouth of the Chikago River emptying into the southwest end of Lake Michigan where a fort formerly stood." With the Louisiana Purchase in 1803 adding vast lands to the west, Henry Dearborn, in his capacity as secretary of war, saw the importance of establishing a communications base for the new territories. Dearborn directed General Jean Francois Hamtramck, in command of the fort at Detroit, "to send a suitable officer with six men and one or two guides across the country to the mouth of St. Josephs [River] at the south end of Lake Michigan and thence to Chikago…to examine the situation with a view to the establishment of a post."

The rest, of course, is Mrs. O'Leary's cow, the world's first skyscraper and the Cubs finally winning a World Series after 108 years—history. Hamtramck's men did find that path (largely present-day U.S. 12, the main Detroit-to-Chicago road until Interstate 94 was built), and they did indeed establish that fort—on the south bank of the Chicago River, about a half

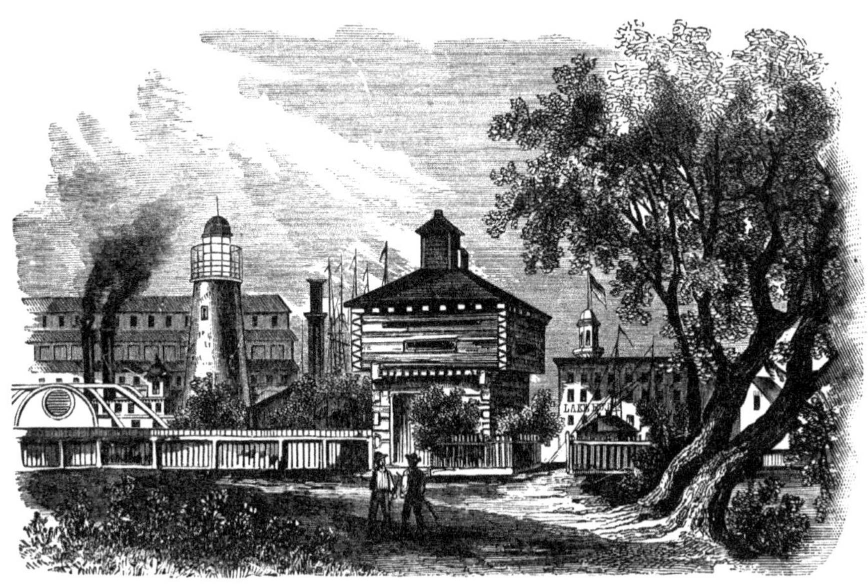

The Last Vestige of Fort Dearborn. From Harper's Encyclopedia of United States History, 1912; *courtesy of Indiana University.*

mile from Lake Michigan. The outpost was named, rightly enough, Fort Dearborn for the man who commissioned it and laid out the plans to make it happen. The fort's first commander was none other than John Whistler, the captured British officer who joined the winning team. The "Chikago" River area had been sparsely inhabited by settlers and traders since the 1780s, but as so often happens with the establishment of a fort, soldiers move in with their families, settlers start to congregate in villages outside the walls and commerce begins to expand. So, while Henry Dearborn did not found Chicago—those early traders did—he *made* Chicago. Dearborn's decision to establish a fort to serve the burgeoning West at the mouth of the Chicago River, with all the attendant population growth and commerce, was the nucleus for the great city that exists today.

In the United States, we have our Uncle Sam, England has its John Bull, New York City has its Father Knickerbocker and likewise Chicago, by the late nineteenth century, came to be personified by "Father Dearborn." Nothing says "you're in the big time" to a place quite like a cartoon character on the local newspaper editorial pages!

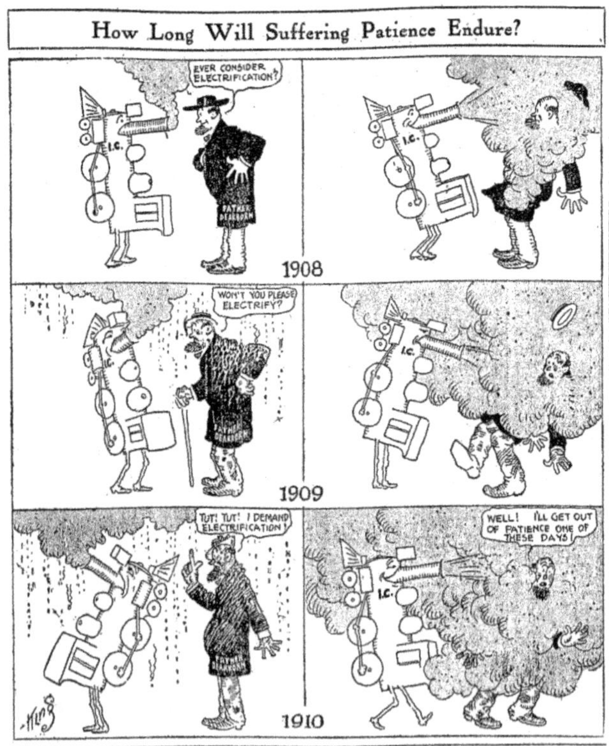

Father Dearborn (unsuccessfully!) takes on the Illinois Central over air pollution in Chicago. *Courtesy of Kevinh.blogspot.com and* Chicago Tribune.

Henry Dearborn is honored at several other locations in the United States as well. Odiorne Park in Rye was established on the site of another Fort Dearborn that existed from 1942 to 1948 as part of the U.S. Army harbor defenses of Portsmouth during the Second World War. The emplacements for the two sixteen-inch guns once there still exist. There is a Dearborn River in Montana (so named by Lewis and Clark on their expedition), a Dearborn County in Indiana and a Dearborn, Missouri. And just for good measure, Augusta, Maine, is named after Dearborn's second daughter.

Thus far, we've seen Henry Dearborn as a doctor, Minuteman, prisoner of war, Revolutionary War hero, congressman, territorial marshal, militia general and secretary of war. He crossed paths with John Stark, George Washington, Benedict Arnold, Aaron Burr and John Whistler. He was married twice and was the father of four children. He put in motion the future city of Chicago. Most folks would have proudly called it a day and retired to the farm. Instead, by 1809, he had moved to Boston and was appointed tax collector for that city and then was chosen by President Madison at the beginning of the War of 1812 to serve as senior major general of the army. His second wife passed away in 1810. Three years later, he married the widowed Sarah Bowdoin, whose husband had been Governor James Bowdoin of Massachusetts—and whose family were benefactors of the well-known Maine college. In 1823, Dearborn was made minister to Portugal by President Monroe. Additionally, the future king of France, Louis Philippe I, in exile at the time, dropped by to visit Henry when he was still living in Maine, and later on, Revolutionary War hero Marquis de Lafayette of France paid him a visit in Boston.

Amazingly, there is another surprising twist to this story. Henry Dearborn is credited with the development of a highly popular vehicle called, logically enough, the Dearborn Wagon. This was a light, four-wheeled vehicle customarily having a top with side and rear curtains, usually pulled by one horse. Whereas the "prairie schooners" used in wagon trains were designed to move an entire family and their possessions out west, Dearborn wagons were more a light-duty excursion vehicle. Typical uses might be for a country doctor on a call, a family going visiting on a Sunday afternoon or an army officer going out to inspect a site. "Dearborns" mostly had one seat, but sometimes as many as two or three, often rested on wooden springs. Later models sometimes had a rear hinged gate and seats that could slide in either direction, making the Dearborn Wagon useful for carrying freight or passengers with baggage. Sounds a lot like a modern station wagon! This vehicle was ubiquitous for most of the nineteenth century, including heavy

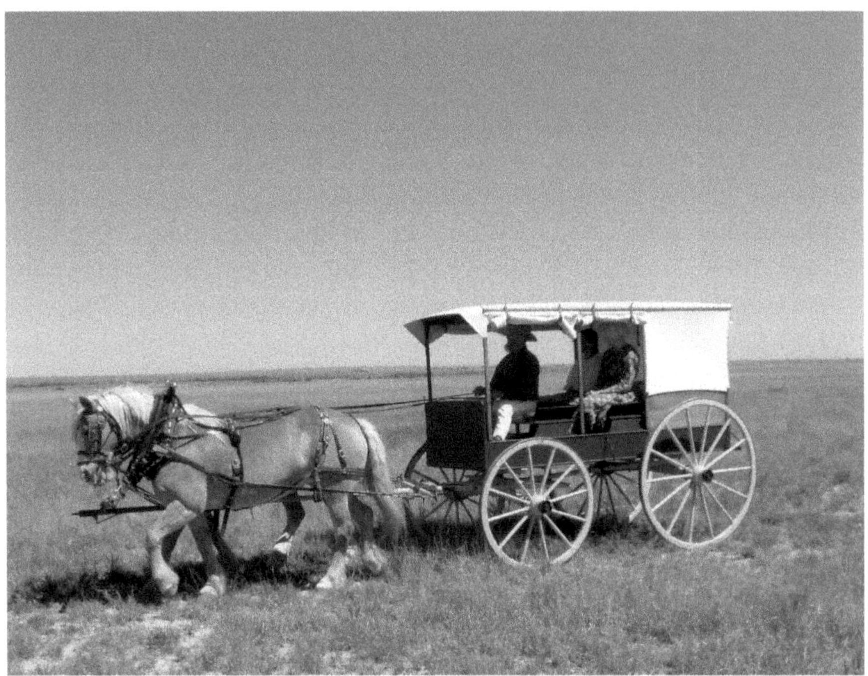

A replica Dearborn wagon at Bent's Old Fort National Historic Site, Colorado. The constructor, Hansen's Wheel & Wagon Shop in South Dakota, had to largely use written descriptions to build it, as there are few known reliable images of a Dearborn. *National Park Service.*

use on the Santa Fe Trail, which is a bit surprising since one would expect a much heavier vehicle would be needed on that arduous journey.

Edward Everett Hale, famed abolitionist and the author of *The Man Without a Country*, wrote in *The Outlook* magazine in 1902: "Observe that no wagon of four wheels for pleasure traveling was known until General Dearborn introduced such a wagon from the West in the period of the English war; and the light four wheeled wagon in which people began to ride from place to place was called the 'Dearborn Wagon.'" It somehow seems fitting that the man who was responsible for a nineteenth-century everyman's vehicle should lend his name to the hometown of the company that brought useful, affordable cars to everyone.

Henry Dearborn passed away peacefully in 1829. In 1940, a prominent Chicago doctor, Frank J. Jirka, published a book called *American Doctors of Destiny: A Collection of Historical Narratives of the Lives of Great American Physicians and Surgeons Whose Service to the Nation and to the World Has Transcended the Scope of Their Profession.* One of the first chapters is dedicated to the story of Dr.

Henry Dearborn. An earlier chapter is devoted to another physician and Patriot, General Joseph Warren, who fell at the Battle of Bunker Hill. At the close of his chapter about Dr. Dearborn, Jirka writes:

> *At Forest Hills Cemetery (in Jamaica Plain) on the summits of two adjoined hills called Mount Warren and Mount Dearborn repose the bones of those two unselfish and brave physicians who so valiantly fought together in the first battle for independence. A deep dell of exquisite loveliness runs between the two heights.*

There certainly is an extraordinary story behind that small monument just off Nottingham Square.

London Bridge, Windham

Not in London, Not a Bridge

I can't believe they're going to hold up the whole project for a pile of rocks!
—*Windham Schools staff member*

Until 2009, the Windham School District had never had its own high school. Located just to the west of Salem, Windham historically tuitioned its high school–age students to Salem High School, with costs eventually running into the millions of dollars per year. As the town's population exploded, nearly doubling from 5,664 in 1980 to 10,859 in 2000, residents realized it was time to build their own high school. In 2005, as the town population neared an estimated 13,000, Windham voters overwhelmingly approved moving the high school project forward. Land was bought, plans were made, architects were hired and engineers were engaged. The 167-acre parcel that was to eventually become the home of the Windham High School Jaguars was located on the south side of NH Route 111. The most logical course to the proposed site from Route 111 was to rebuild a long-closed section of London Bridge Road (following closely, but not precisely, the original road) from which an access road to the high school would be built. Therein lay the problem.

Impressive architectural renderings of the proposed $44 million project had been made public, and there was much excitement among the townsfolk and school employees about the prospect of having their own brand spanking new high school. Teachers were especially excited about how wonderfully the students would be served in the new state-of-the-

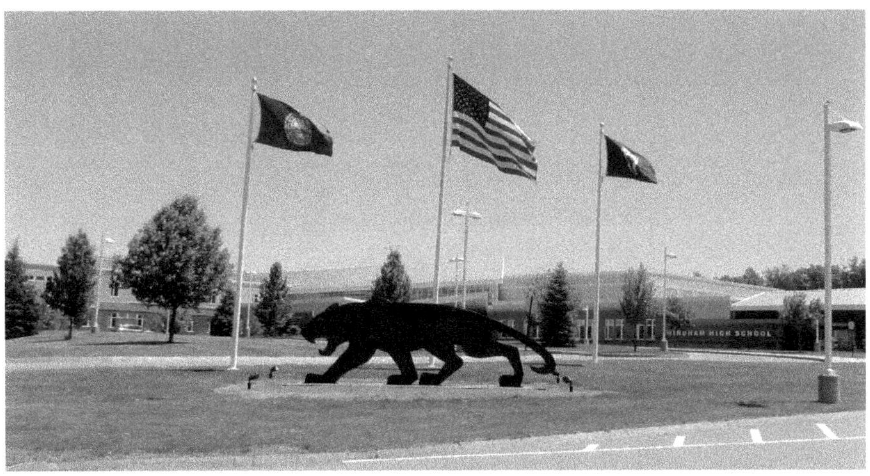

Windham High School, home of the Jaguars. *Author's photo.*

art building. The planned opening of the high school was to be in 2008, coinciding with the end of the tuition agreement with Salem. In a March 2006 meeting of district educators, the subject was brought up of a recent *Boston Globe* article regarding the potential halting of the project due to the fact that an old stone causeway lay directly in the path of the school's proposed access road. One member of that group was heard to exclaim, "I can't believe they're going to hold up the whole project for a pile of rocks!"

Windham was also growing in the 1790s. In 1798, a new meetinghouse was built in what would become Windham's town center. There was a need for new roads to connect outlying farms to the town center, which was located on today's Route 111. At a town meeting held on December 16, 1799, several new roads were approved. One was described in the town records thus:

> *Road leading from Dea. William Gregg's running easterly by an old road where two roads meet, then marked by trees to a rock by the side of a gut* [a gully through which water passes] *that must be bridged; then by marked trees to where there has been an old coal-pit; then through Mr. Joseph Clyde's pasture, crossing a small brook, at an old ford, and out the north of said Clyde's house, to a road leading from James Clark's house to Captain Clyde's. Three rods wide* [49.5 feet].

And so the road was built, commerce flowed and the structure that bridges the gut, frankly, does pretty much look like a "pile of rocks." But

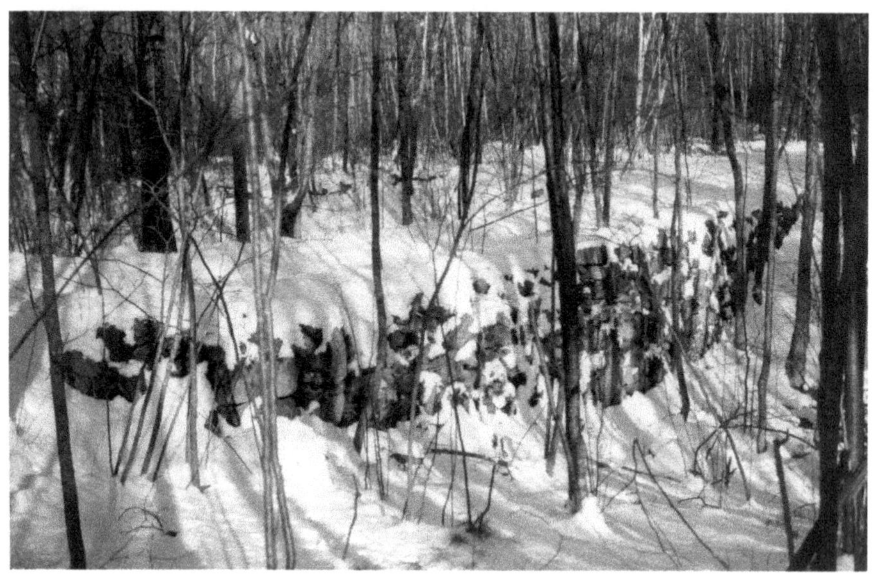

The London Bridge Causeway. *Courtesy of the New Hampshire Division of Historical Resources.*

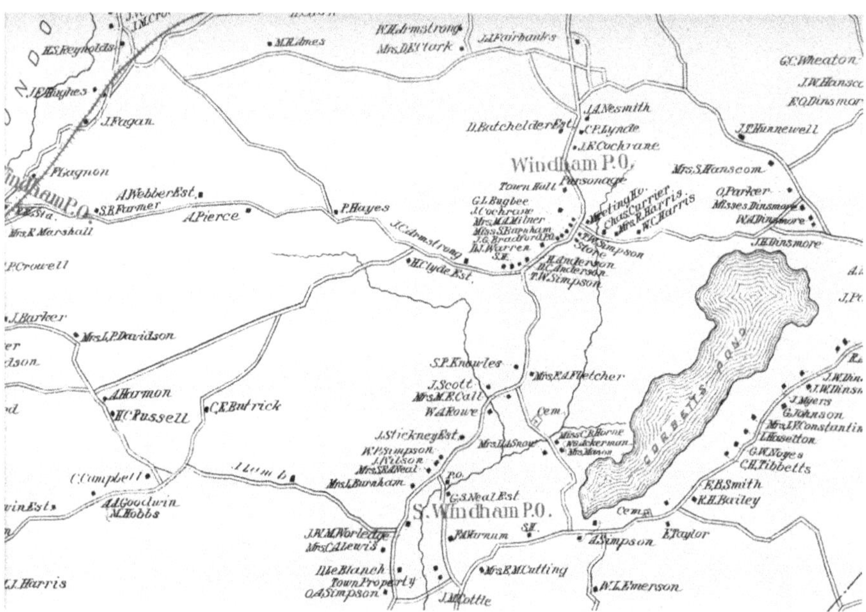

Windham, 1892, by D.H. Hurd. North is at the top. London Bridge Road runs southwest from "H. Clyde's" place, near the center of the map, passing "C.E. Butrick's" place. The causeway was just to the southwest of where the road crosses the stream. "J.C. Armstrong's" place is on the current Route 111. *Courtesy of the Windham Historical Commission.*

as so often happens in life, looks can be deceiving. This particular pile of rocks turned out to be a causeway (a sort of embankment that carries a road across low or wet ground, as opposed to a bridge, which supports a roadway between piers) about ten feet high, one hundred feet long and somewhat narrower than originally planned. And as it turns out, it was a pretty significant one, historically.

When the district's engineers were planning the access road from the new London Bridge Road to the high school, they chose the same spot to bridge the gut that the original planners had chosen in 1799. The plan was to demolish the causeway, which was known locally as London Bridge, to make way for the high school access road. As Windham Historical District Committee member Carol Pynn explained in the *Globe* article, "It was the best way to get there in 1799 and I guess it's still the best way in 2006."

Now, in the scheme of things, this isn't quite as big of a deal as a similar situation described in Douglas Adams's *Hitchhiker's Guide to the Galaxy*, where the Galactic Hyperspace Planning Council plans to demolish Earth in order to make room for a new express space route. But to Pynn and many others, it was still a pretty big deal. Big enough to stop the entire high school project (and jeopardize the planned school opening date) so that studies could be made to determine if London Bridge qualified as eligible for the National Register of Historic Places and therefore protected from demolition.

About the same time as the district started planning the new high school, a local hunter named Bill Duggan mentioned to his friend Pynn and other members of the Windham Historical District Committee that there was an old stone structure in the woods. It was in an area where he frequently hunted and near where the new high school was to be built. He drove them out to the site in his four-wheeler to see for themselves, and the committee members immediately recognized a structure with the potential to be historically important. This turned out to be the London Bridge Causeway. The committee informed the school district of its concerns about the potential destruction of the causeway in the high school access road plans. It also contacted the Federal Highway Administration, which invoked a federal regulation known as Section 106 that basically held that new roadways must take into account their impact on historical resources. As a result, several studies were ordered. The district expressed concern that the effort to protect the causeway would cause significant delays in the opening of the school and could cost hundreds of thousands of extra dollars.

Dr. James Garvin, New Hampshire architectural historian, directed the studies, which included input from various state, local and UNH sources,

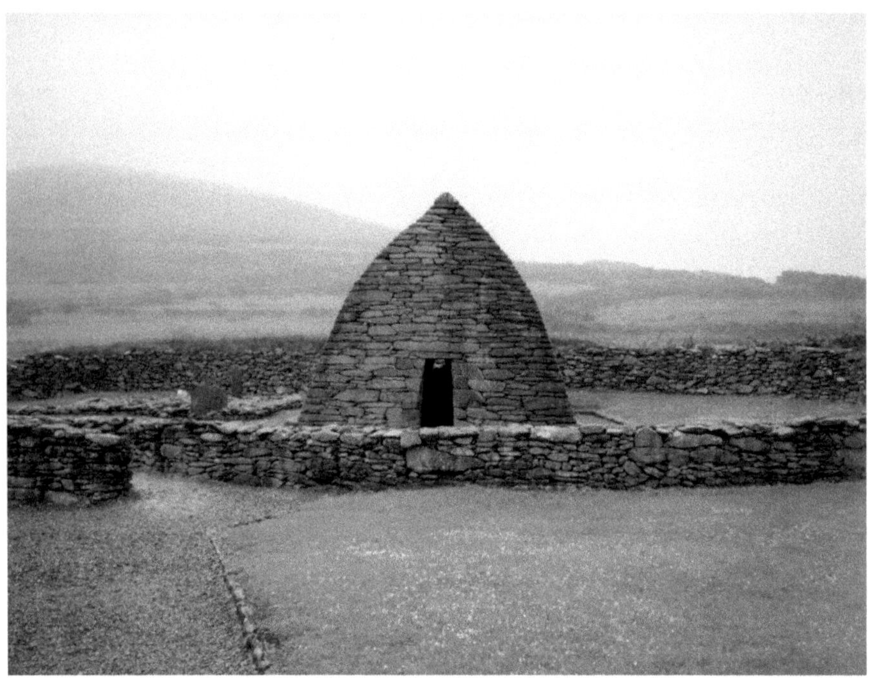

The Gallarus Oratory on Ireland's Dingle Peninsula—an outstanding example of Irish dry laid stone construction. Still waterproof after more than nine hundred years! *Photo by Barbara Nelson.*

as well as private consultants. The findings state that the causeway is a type of construction called dry laid stone, a very sturdy style that does not use mortar. Indeed, the use of mortar in such a structure can be detrimental due to its rigidity, and therefore, weaknesses can develop in the structure.

Since the early Windham settlers were largely Scotch-Irish, dry laid stone building techniques would have been very familiar to them. The reports go on to say that dry laid stone structures such as London Bridge Causeway are extremely strong, capable of bearing loads far in excess of what would have been originally expected, and are durable even in the face of seismic activity. Although at one time there were many such structures in New Hampshire, there are now only three others known to exist: one in Canterbury, one in Wilton and one in Kensington known as the Dearborn Road Causeway. Could this be yet another landmark named for our famous Nottingham general?

Not this time. As it turns out, this Dearborn Road, with its causeway, was named for an ancestor of Henry Dearborn who settled a farm that still exists next to the road. A subsequent owner of the property inscribed the

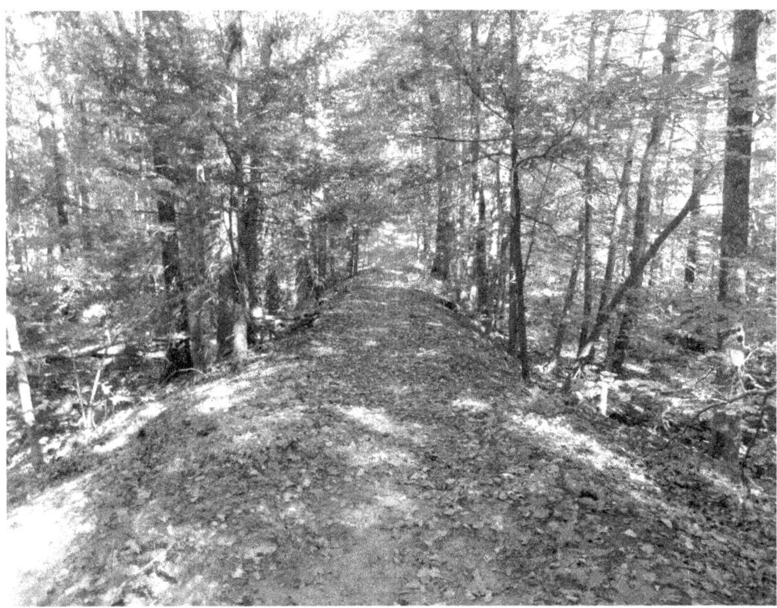

The inviting path on the Dearborn Causeway, Kensington. *Author's photo.*

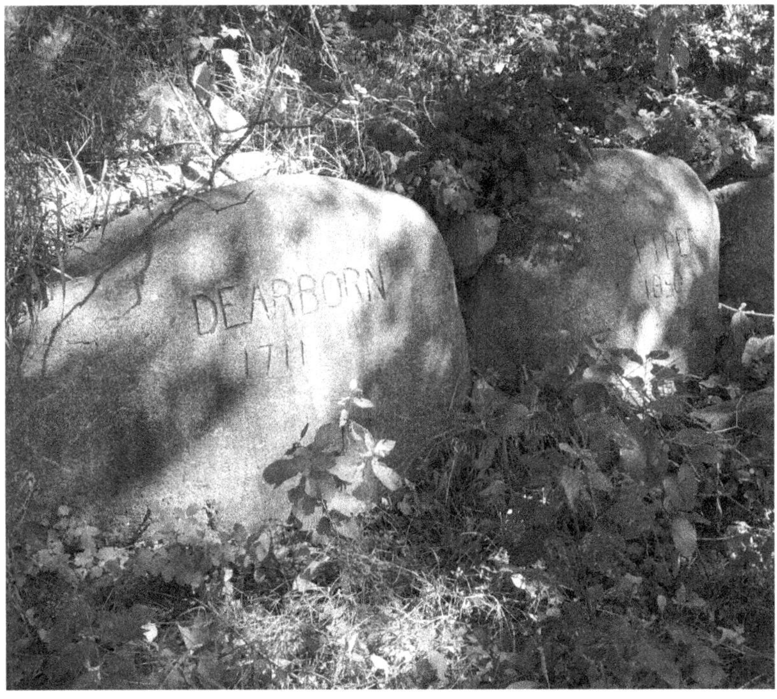

The engraved stone displaying Dearborn family ownership of a farm in Kensington. *Author's photo.*

names of all the previous owners on rocks lining the roadway—showing that this Dearborn bought his land in 1711, forty years before General Dearborn's birth.

Meanwhile, back in Windham, Dr. Garvin produced the findings. He writes that the causeway "is a rare, intact example of early road construction in…Windham and provides important information about late-eighteenth and early nineteenth century development of transportation routes across the town"; "is a well-preserved example of late-eighteenth to early-nineteenth century road related construction"; "is relatively uncommon in that most causeways were constructed of logs, rock and earth"; and "maintains a high degree of integrity of location, design, setting, materials, workmanship, feeling and association." He sums up by saying, "Windham's causeway represents an immense investment in labor in an age when less permanent road construction was the rule….The London Bridge Road causeway was never altered, leaving the structure as a museum piece of early transportation history." In the *Boston Globe* article, Dr. Garvin added, "This took a huge amount of effort by men and animals, to pull these boulders into place one by one. We understand the difficulty to the community, but this could be a valuable lesson for students."

Based on these findings, the New Hampshire Division of Historical Resources on February 8, 2006, determined that the London Bridge Road Causeway was indeed eligible to be listed in the National Register of Historic Places, declaring, "The causeway is eligible for its significance in history, engineering, and for its potential to yield important information about the construction of these types of structures."

Game, set, match…the causeway stands today, with the Windham High School access road curving safely around it.

Now, one might think this is the end of a happy story—albeit one that cost the Windham taxpayers a pile of dough to save that important pile of rocks. But another really nice thing came out of this little saga. Not long after the high school access road was built, but while the building was still under construction, Nick Letizio, a local Boy Scout looking to attain his Eagle status, noticed the causeway forlornly fenced in with trash strewn about the area. He decided that making the London Bridge Causeway a place of beauty, rest and reflection would be his Eagle project.

To become an Eagle Scout is akin to a very long-term graduate school project. It is the highest of seven levels of scouting one must pass through to earn that coveted Eagle badge. Gerald Ford, Neil Armstrong (and at least thirty-nine other astronauts!), Stephen Spielberg, Michael Bloomberg,

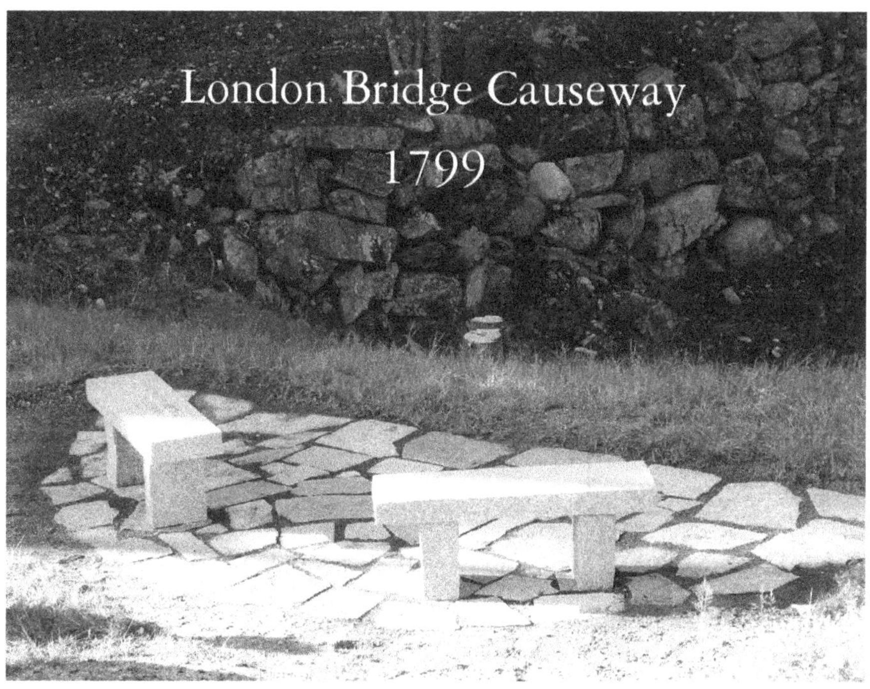

Nick's finished Eagle project. *Courtesy of Nick Letizio.*

former Red Sox Shane Victorino, Michael Dukakis, former Texas governor Rick Perry, former New Hampshire senator Warren Rudman and *The Simpsons* writer and producer George Meyer were all Eagle Scouts. Along the way, the scout must earn at least twenty-one merit badges and then come up with and execute his Eagle project. A plan of action with detailed steps, procurement of materials and necessary tools, fundraising, physical completion of the project and a final meeting with the troop scoutmaster must be completed prior to a final presentation made before the district council Eagle Board of Review. All but the Board of Review presentation must be finished by the scout's eighteenth birthday before the Eagle badge can be awarded. Nick's project turned out beautifully. The site is clean and the causeway is honored. It provides a restful spot where Windham High School students, or anyone else, can visit and indeed reflect on Windham's history, the people who built and used the causeway and how it helped to shape modern Windham.

And how on earth did this "pile of rocks" get named London Bridge? The simple answer, regretfully, is that no one knows for sure. The first reference to the name doesn't appear in any records until the 1880s—and that one

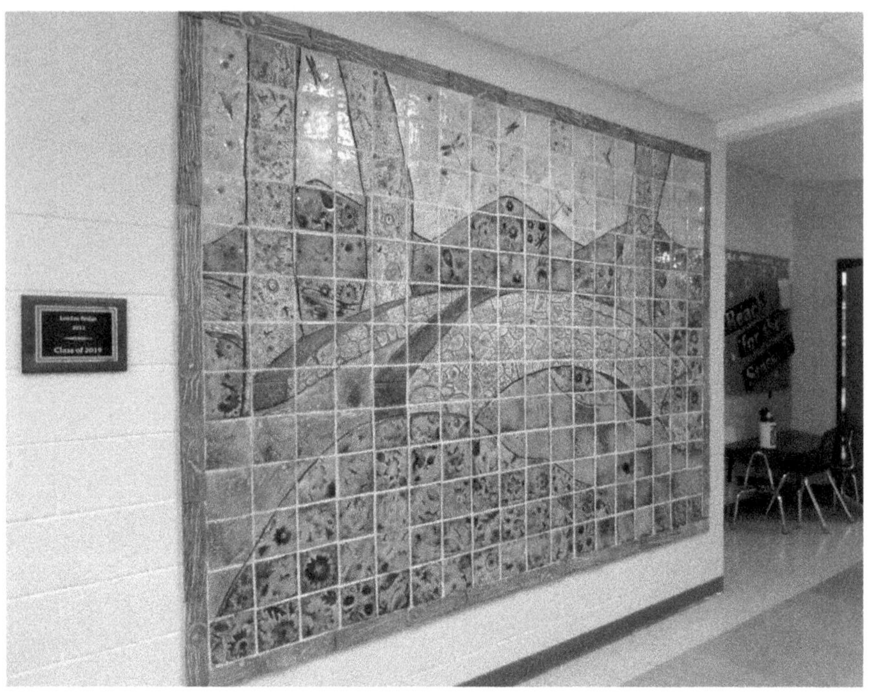

The London Bridge mosaic at the Windham Center School. *Author's photo with permission.*

doesn't speak to why London Bridge was so named. Nick reports that the townsfolk he spoke with about his project surmised that it may have been that the difficult-to-maintain structure kept "falling down" (not literally, but the heavy wagons frequently using it would occasionally cause stones to fall out) so the early residents gave it the wry name of "London Bridge."

There's yet one more happy turn to this story. For many years, the fifth graders at the Windham Center School have followed a tradition of erecting mosaics throughout the building honoring important sites around Windham as a class gift to their school. In 2012, the Center School fifth graders (the future Windham High School class of 2019) chose the London Bridge Causeway as their project. These are all-class projects wherein every student helps to make the tiles. As can be seen in the picture above (and acknowledging that the bridge in the mosaic is perhaps a bit on the stylized side since flowing water never actually ran under the structure), one can't deny its beauty and meaning. It is wonderful to see this school embrace a subject that, not too many years before, was so controversial. From town necessity, to near destruction, to place of honor—circle complete.

Little Boar's Head

Take her up! The inductions open!
—*USS* Squalus *crew member*

The drive down Ocean Boulevard from Odiorne Point to Hampton is one of the most pleasant in our state. In addition to the wonderful views of the ever-changing ocean, the drive features beautiful beaches, grand homes and great seafood restaurants. Tucked in between are lots of small cottages and bathhouses. Pulling into the parking lot of North Hampton State Park provides, in addition to views of the beautiful ocean and the occasional surfer, a chance to visit one of New England's most unusual hidden treasures. Walking north from your car along the coast, you encounter a little pocket garden next to an inviting path with a small sign that reads "King's Highway." Several intriguing cottages lie just beyond. Close to the cottages, there is an informational sign erected by the local Heritage Commission labeled "The Fish Houses at Little Boar's Head." The sign goes on to explain that there had been fish houses at this spot since at least 1804 and that they were used by fishermen to store their equipment. That fact would be easy to miss from the road because they pretty much look like the other little seaside cottages one passes by.

As can be seen in the vintage photo, the fish houses originally were anything but summer cottages. The first mention of them was in 1804, when the selectmen of North Hampton were petitioned to "build a road to the fish houses" from the village center, thus establishing that at least some of them

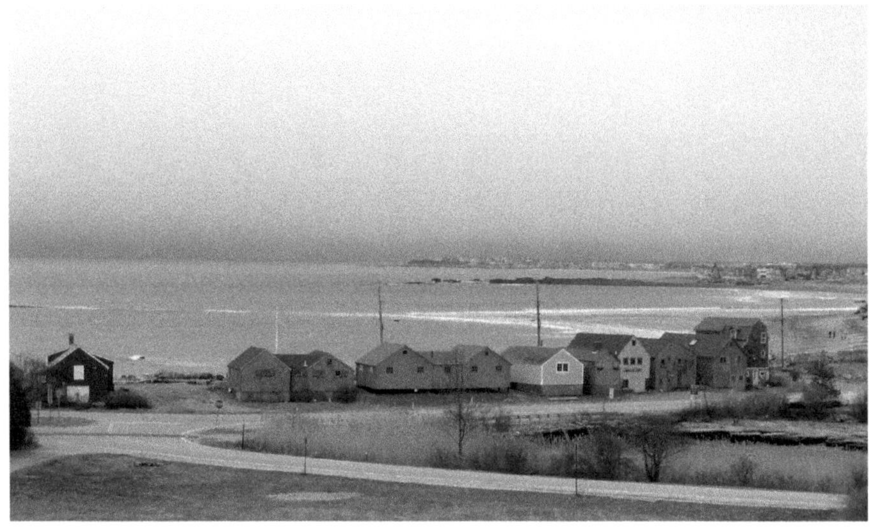

The North Hampton fish houses, backing up to Ocean Avenue, viewed from the Little Boar's Head drumlin. *Author's photo.*

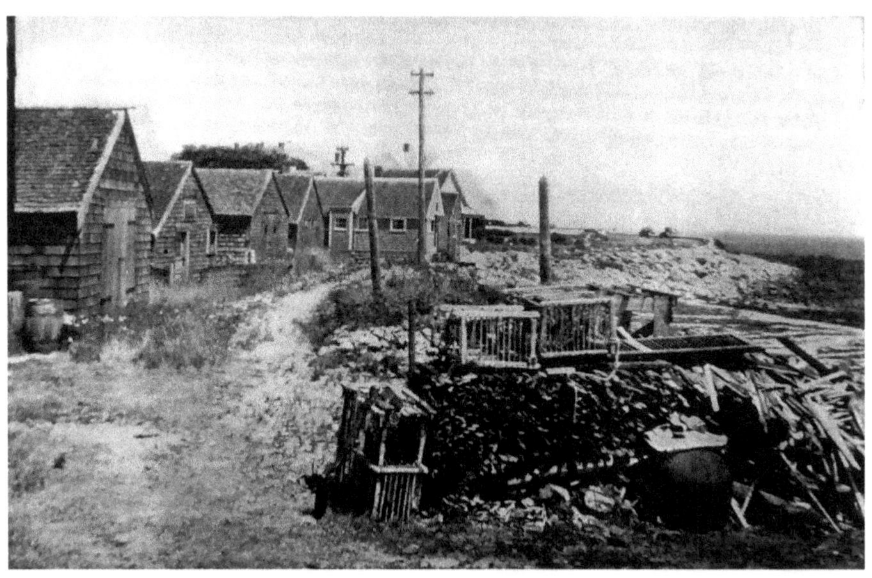

North Hampton fish houses seven through twelve, probably around 1940. *Courtesy of the Historic District Commission of the Village District of Little Boar's Head.*

were in existence by that time. Such a road was necessary in part because there was no Ocean Boulevard (today's Route 1-A) at that time. Some of the fishermen who used these houses were local farmers who would fish during the winter to supplement their incomes. In their fish house, they would store tools of their trade such as lines, nets, sails and traps while keeping their dories on the shore in front of the house.

Old maps show the King's Highway running through Cape Arundel in Kennebunkport, Maine, and anyone who has spent time at the ocean in Goose Rocks Beach (a Kennebunkport village) may have noticed that the road by the beach is also called the King's Highway. Additionally, the King's Highway stretches for about a mile just off the beach in Hampton. Those 150 yards or so of pathway in front of the fish houses were an original part of a road that eventually stretched from Portland to Savannah, Georgia. This road was ordered by King Charles II in 1664 to link the colonies from Boston to Charles Towne (now Charleston), South Carolina. Over the years, the route extended to Portland and Savannah, Georgia.

The part of the King's Highway in front of the fish houses could be much earlier. In 1905, Langdon B. Parsons wrote in his *History of the Town of Rye*, "There was a road or pathway along the seashore from Portsmouth through Rye to Hampton as early as 1644." According to a 1970 Maine Highway Commission report, in 1653, the Massachusetts Colony Crown Commissioners ordered the building of "sufficient roads" along the shore from Kittery to Portland, thereby enabling officials to travel to the province of Maine (then a part of Massachusetts) to hold court. That 1970 report goes on to point out that despite the high-sounding name, an early stretch of the road was nothing more than "two wheel ruts with a horse path in between." That description would certainly explain the narrow path in front of the fish houses.

There are other "King's Highways" in New Hampshire, including in Merrimack and Lebanon. According to *Collins English Dictionary*, in Britain (which was, of course, us for a while) a King's—or Queen's—Highway is defined as "any public road or highway," so it's not surprising that that there are several roads so named in our state. Ironically, the term is not used for any major roads in Britain, but it is the name used for all provincial highways in Ontario, Canada. Eventually, the collection of roads that made up that first King's Highway, including the portion running in front of the fish houses, was rerouted inland and straightened, becoming today's U.S. Route 1. But if you take a walk along that little stretch of highway in front of the fish houses, you will be walking in the footsteps that our earliest European settlers trod over 370 years ago.

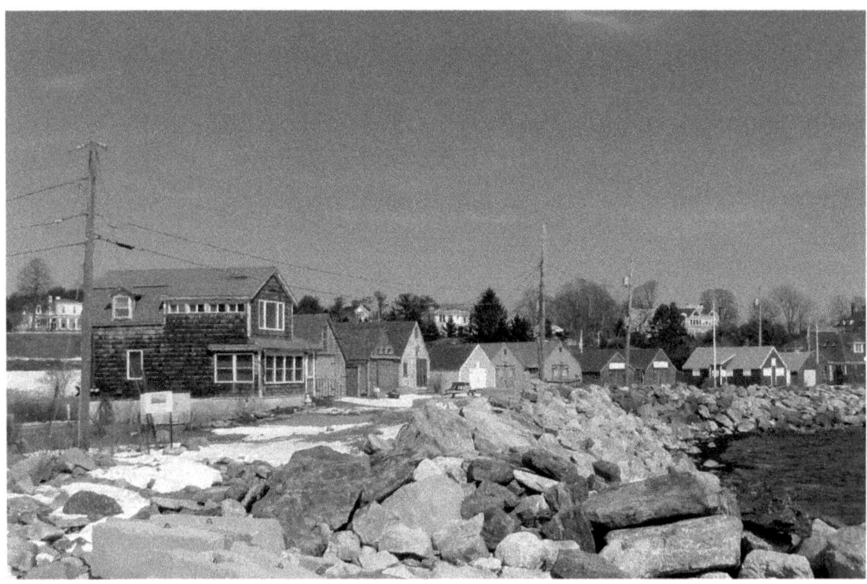

The North Hampton fish houses with the King's Highway running in front of them. Fish house five is too far back to be seen. *Author's photo.*

Little Boar's Head is a village district of North Hampton (the birthplace of one Henry Dearborn!). The area was named by seventeenth-century English surveyors who named two drumlins (elongated hills formed by glacial movement) they had seen from the ocean "Great Bores-hed" (three miles south in what is now Hampton) and "Little Bores-hed." In 1994, the Little Boar's Head Historic District Commission produced a detailed history in advance of a successful petition to have the entire district listed in the National Register of Historic Places. In the report, the histories of the individual fish houses as well as the other historic properties in the district were cited. For purposes of identification, the committee assigned numbers to each fish house, ranging from number one (the two-story house on the left in the contemporary photo above) to number twelve (with the big white door on the far right). House number five cannot be seen in this image because it is blocked from view by house four, but it can be clearly seen in the photo of the fish houses at the start of this story. The dating of the individual fish houses is imprecise because in the nineteenth century they were of little monetary value and ownership records are a bit sketchy. The Historic District Commission did a great job of piecing together as much history of each as possible.

Fish house number one is the only one with an upper floor. Dating from sometime before 1900, it saw duty as a bathhouse before it was moved across the road to its present location. **Fish houses two and three** are both from the mid- to late nineteenth century. **Fish house four** predates 1875. In 1945, it was bought by Oliver Henkel, the last fisherman to use the houses for their original purpose. Born in Norway in 1882, when Henkel came to the United States, he started out as a chauffeur for one of the prominent families of the area. He switched to fishing for a living in 1917, working out of house number three until he bought number four. When not busy catching lobster, Henkel served as the town's only police officer. He retired from fishing in 1956—the last lobsterman on the coast. **Fish house five** is the smallest of the houses, which explains why it can't be seen in the photo. It was built by a gentleman named Oliver Fogg sometime in the late nineteenth century.

Fish house six is one of the oldest houses, being built in 1840. Its chief claim to fame is that during the historic nor'easter of February 7–9, 1978, it was pushed off its foundation and deposited in the middle of Ocean Boulevard. Despite the half-billion-dollar damage done by that storm throughout the Northeast, fish house six sustained no damage—not even any broken windows! What saved number six, and likely several other fish houses over the decades, is the fact that they are very well built—using triangular braces in the corners—and they also can float like boats. **Fish houses seven and eight** are a complex of two houses. These are the newest fish houses, built as sort of a duplex in 1947 on the site of two earlier individual houses from the late nineteenth century.

Fish houses nine and ten also form a complex. Originally, they were separate houses built around 1900. In the 1940s, celebrated New York sculptor Malvina Hoffman joined the two houses together and used them as her summer studio. This was the first time the fish houses were used for something other than their original purpose. Hoffman had been spending summers at Little Boar's Head with her family from New York since she was a child. Her father was a renowned concert pianist from England who had been brought to America by none other than P.T. Barnum as an accompanist for singer Jenny "The Swedish Nightingale" Lind. Growing up in an artistic household, Malvina began to show talent in painting but soon turned her attention toward sculpture. She honed her craft studying under legendary French sculptor Auguste Rodin—he of *The Thinker*—and Gutzon Borglum, sculptor of Mount Rushmore. While in Paris with Rodin, Hoffman's circle of friends included famed pianist and Polish patriot Ignacy Jan Paderewski, legendary dancer Anna Pavlova and Impressionist painter Claude Monet. Rodin taught her that, among other things, sculpting was

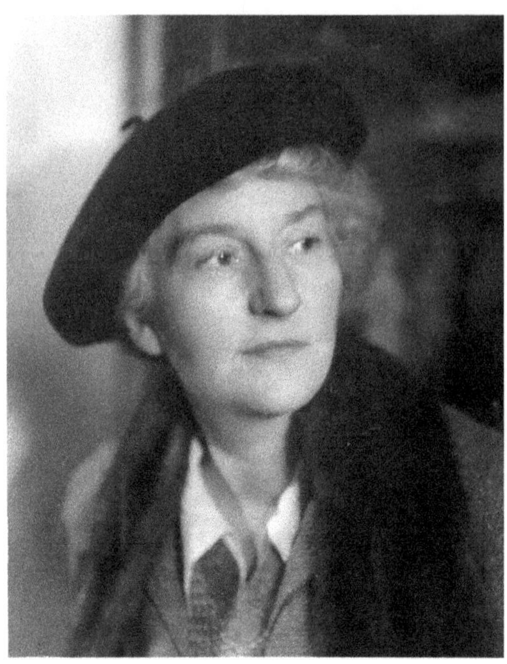

Malvina Hoffman. *Smithsonian Institution photo.*

physically demanding and that she had to become used to lifting heavy objects. As such, Hoffman learned to use carpenter's and plumber's tools and to bend iron, saw wood and design and build the frameworks around which a sculpture is crafted. She became expert on the physics of materials and learned to calculate the stresses and strengths necessary to create her heavy works of art.

Hoffman soon became renowned in her own right. Perhaps her greatest work was commissioned by Stanley Field, nephew of department store magnate Marshall Field and director of the Field Museum of Natural History in Chicago. In 1929, Field asked Hoffman to sculpt and cast bronze figures depicting the peoples of the world. At a time when very few people could afford to visit other lands, Field's idea was to "use sculpture as a way to reveal man to his brother." Hoffman traveled the world for several years, meeting with various groups of people and creating statues. The result was *The Races of Mankind*—104 sculptures in bronze placed in the Field Museum's Hall of Man. The exhibit ran from 1935 until her death in 1966, but in 2016, the Field Museum again displayed fifty works from *The Races of Mankind.* Closer to home, in 1923, Hoffman created *The Sacrifice* for Harvard University's World War I Memorial Chapel (now called Harvard Memorial Church). After World War II, she created relief sculptures for the memorial at the American Cemetery in Vosges, France, site of the Battle of the Bulge.

During both wars, she served as a Red Cross volunteer. Fish houses nine and ten were badly damaged by a fire in 1994 but were quickly restored.

According to the report of the National Register of Historic Places Commission, **fish houses eleven and twelve** were both built around 1850. Number eleven was owned by Elias Card, who fished from it until 1929, making him the second-to-last lobsterman on the shore. That means that Officer Oliver Henkel soldiered on by himself for twenty-seven years as the last fisherman. The owner of number twelve, Mary Frye Frost, allowed Card to store his equipment there during the winter months. During World War II, the local Red Cross would hold regular meetings there. If you visit the fish houses, you will see a lovely garden on the north side of them. This garden was the idea of Mrs. Frost, and she planted the first flowers there.

North Hampton was not the only seacoast town to have had fish houses. Less than a mile down the road, in Hampton, there were at one time sixteen similar houses. Unfortunately, controversy and litigation have reduced that number down to two today. In 1950, thirteen "fish houses" were still left on Hampton's North Beach. The quotation marks are there because some of them were never used as fish houses, and by then, only a couple were still

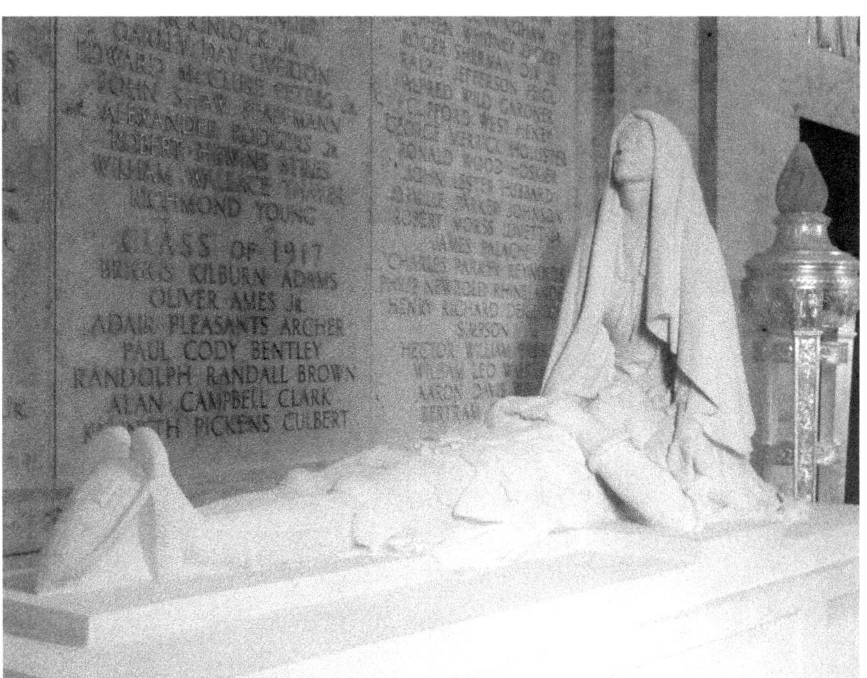

Hoffman's *The Sacrifice* at the Harvard Memorial Church. *Author's photo.*

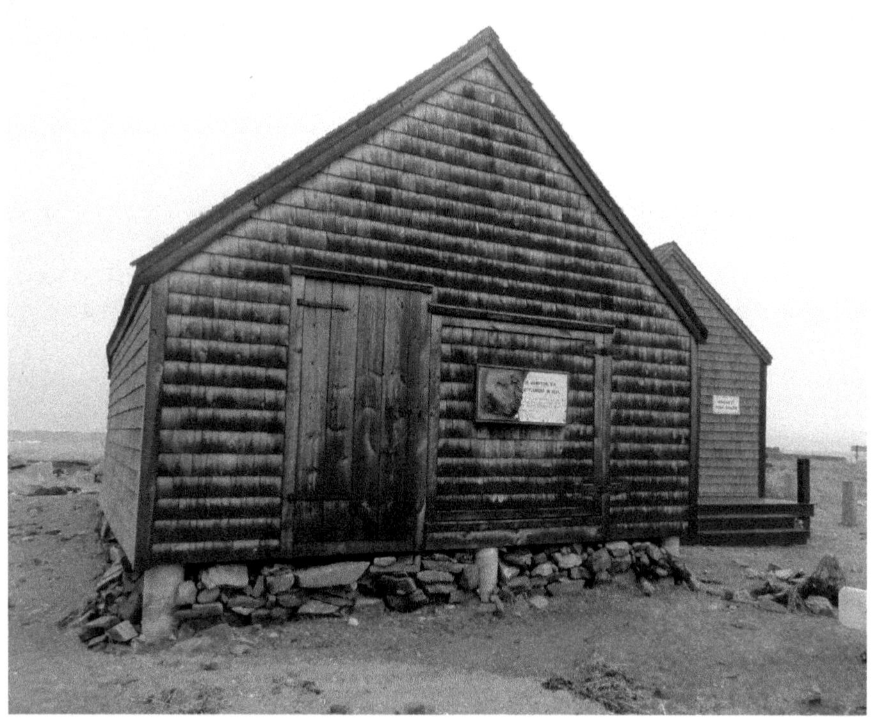

The Mace (on the left) and Doggett fish houses, Hampton. *Author's photo.*

being used for that purpose. Mostly, the houses were used for recreational cottages. What they had in common, however, was that they were all on land that led to a major lawsuit.

The fish houses had been largely left alone by the town when, in 1947, a gentleman wanted to build a house on the land on which his fish house stood. He had owned the building on that site since 1921 and now intended to put up a second building, but the town challenged the new construction. The town wanted to make the area the houses occupied into a recreation area. As such, in 1950, the town notified the owners of the thirteen fish houses that they must be removed. In 1959, after much litigation and many appeals, the New Hampshire Supreme Court ruled for the town, finding that it had owned the land under the fish houses since 1638. The bottom line, the judge ruled, was that over the years, the house owners had conveyed the property for other than fishing and that had contravened the tacit agreement that the town would allow the fish houses on public land as long as fishing was going on. As a result, all but two of the houses were removed. The two left, owned by Harold Mace and Arthur Doggett, were allowed to remain because they were still being used for fishing. These are the two Hampton fish houses remaining to this day—sort of.

In 1960, the town decided to make the fish house area a public park, now called the Ruth G. Stimson Park, after a dedicated town conservationist. In 1988, Mace's house was donated to the town while the Doggett house remained with the family. In 2003, a local businessman bought the house from Barbara Doggett. His initial plan was to preserve the building, but he decided that it could not be saved. In 2007, he made the decision to demolish it and build a replica. As it turned out, the town had not given him permission to tear down the original building; he had only been given permits to restore it. Not surprisingly, a lot of controversy ensued. Preservationist-minded folks felt that he had no right to tear down the original building, especially considering that it had been done without the town's permission, and they felt that the replica should be demolished as well. Others felt that the older building was an eyesore and the new replica was an improvement. The matter went to the town council, which eventually ruled that the new building could stay.

One can't drive down that stretch of Ocean Boulevard in North Hampton without admiring the beautiful homes lining the other side of the road from the fish houses. Among the many projects initiated by President Franklin Delano Roosevelt during the Great Depression was a series of travel books written by the Workers of the Federal Writers' Project called the American Guide Series. The purpose of this project was to provide work for unemployed writers. At a time when unemployment reached 25 percent of the workforce, there were several different programs meant to get people working again. Dozens of these projects were in New Hampshire, including the building of roads, bridges, libraries and schools and the creation of murals. One of those federal projects was Spaulding High School in Rochester, built in 1939. In 2017, it was named by *Architectural Digest* magazine as New Hampshire's most beautiful public high school as part of a feature naming such schools in each state.

In the Dover library history room, there is a 1938 book from the American Guide Series titled *New Hampshire: A Guide to the Granite State*, in which the chapters are set up as various road trips around the state. One such journey, driving north from Seabrook to Portsmouth on Ocean Boulevard, includes this entry: "Little Boar's Head...a precinct of North Hampton, is the show place of eastern New Hampshire. Approaching it from the south and rounding the curve in the road appear in order the Studebaker estate, and the Nutting, Fuller, Spaulding, Manning and Studebaker Mansions."

Two governors are among those well-to-do folks listed in between the two Studebakers in the description above. Governors Alvin Fuller of Massachusetts (1925–29) and Huntley Spaulding of New Hampshire (1927–28) had places next door to each other on Ocean Boulevard. Huntley's brother Rolland also served as New Hampshire governor from 1915 through 1917. Both are from Rochester, hence the high school's name. While Huntley Spaulding's mansion still exists, Fuller's was torn down in 1961. Thankfully, the beautiful gardens commissioned by Governor Fuller in the 1920s still exist and are open to the public.

As it turns out, these stately homes were once part of a high society "summer colony." In 1862, Mary Bell White, daughter of U.S. senator James Bell of New Hampshire, built the first house meant to be a summer "cottage" at Little Boar's Head (the summer crowd used the nickname "LBH"). A few

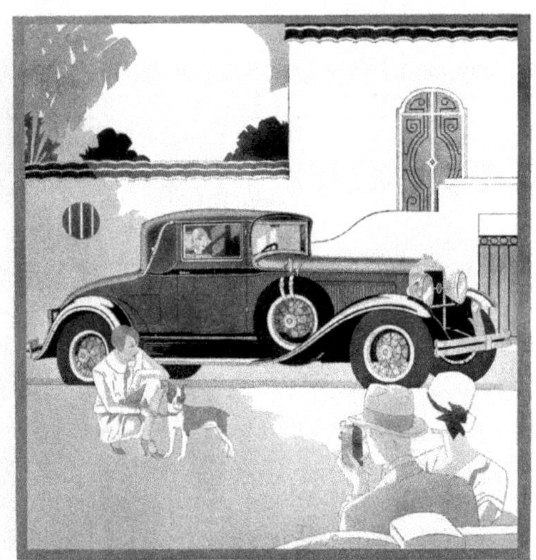

The New President Eight Convertible Cabriolet for Four—six wire wheels and trunk rack standard equipment—$1895 at the factory. Bumpers and spare tires extra

ARTIST and artisan—craftsman and engineer—have struck that rare, keen note of happy harmony in Studebaker's great new eights and sixes. Championship performance, which has won and holds *every* official stock car record for speed and endurance, has been mated with youthful, sophisticated style. Suave and silken power is matched by travel ease. Sturdiness, heroically proved, is linked with perfect manners—obedient to a whim. Each phase thus brilliantly interprets all others in these champions that look—and act—the part!

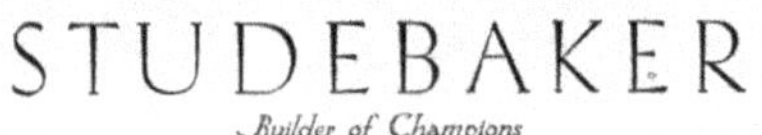

A Studebaker magazine ad from 1929. The house may be Hollywood, but the fashions could absolutely be Little Boar's Head summer colony. *Author's collection.*

years later, in 1868, Albert Batchelder, from a longtime North Hampton family, built a resort hotel there, thus beginning the change in the area from a farming and fishing place to a recreational and residential place. Soon the powerful and the wealthy began to spend their summer "season" on that little stretch of seaside. Over the years, Presidents James Garfield, Chester Allen Arthur, William Taft and Franklin Roosevelt visited Little Boar's Head, either as guests of residents or staying at Batchelder's Hotel. Other visitors included a raft of governors and senators, several railroad presidents, poet Ogden Nash, Houghton Mifflin president Henry O. Houghton and, of course, Malvina Hoffman.

Another member of the summer colony was Alice Hobson, wife of Arthur Hobson, a paper company heir. In the 1930s, Mrs. Hobson established an outdoor summer concert series, called the New Hampshire Seacoast Music Festivals, on the grounds of her estate on Chapel Road. Drawing crowds as large as 2,500, this series was a precursor to current outdoor concert series such as Tanglewood. On July 30, 1939, the Boston Symphony Orchestra, under the direction of Arthur Fiedler, performed a special concert there—one that was not just for entertainment.

Just over two months earlier, on May 23, 1939, the newly commissioned submarine USS *Squalus* left the Portsmouth Naval Shipyard and headed out for sea trials (*Squalus* is Latin for shark). When the *Squalus* reached a position about thirteen miles off the New Hampshire coast, past the Isles of Shoals, skipper Lieutenant Oliver Naquin gave the order to dive. Moments after Naquin's order, a frightening plea from the engine room came over the intercom: "Take her up! The induction's open!" The induction tubes are large intakes designed to feed air to the sub's diesel engines, which power the ship while on the surface, and the tubes also provide fresh ventilation. When submerged, submarines use a self-contained ventilation system while batteries, charged while surface running, power the engines. Some of these tubes were as much as three feet in diameter, and as such, a tremendous amount of water began pouring in. Twenty-six brave sailors were immediately lost when their compartments flooded with no means of escape. Thirty-three men, however, were alive and safe, at least for the time being. Four of the ship's seven compartments were flooded, causing the *Squalus* to sink rapidly. When it hit bottom, it was 240 feet beneath the surface.

Up until that time, no successful submarine rescue had ever occurred at a depth of over twenty feet. Fortunately, Lieutenant Naquin had managed to send up some smoke rockets and a telephone line attached to a buoy.

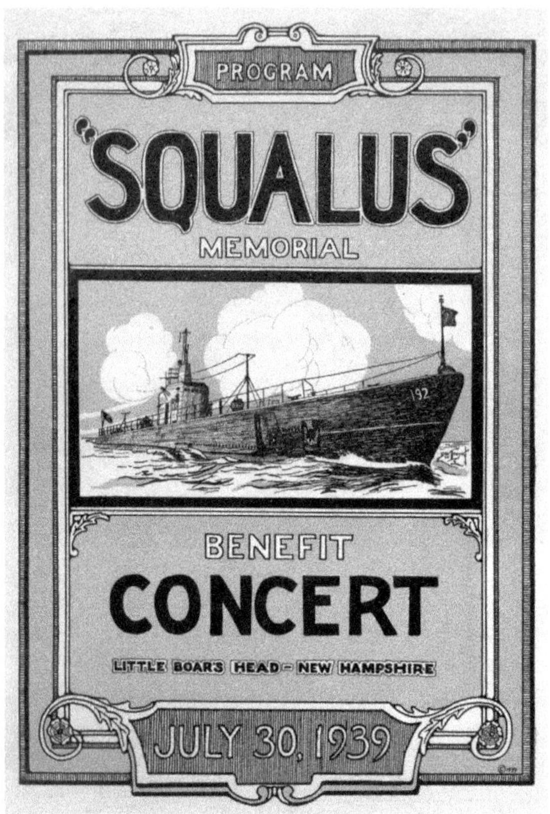

USS *Squalus* memorial concert program cover. *Courtesy of the Tuck Museum, Hampton.*

When the *Squalus* was finally located by its sister ship, the USS *Sculpin*, the captains were able to greet each other over the phone line—until the line broke after just a few seconds. Eventually, an anchor and line were dragged across the crippled sub, and the crews were able to communicate by banging out messages in Morse code. By this time, the *Squalus*'s sinking was making national news. Reportedly, WBZ was first on the scene at the shipyard, where frequent updates were being given. But it wasn't long before people across America were glued to their radios following the dramatic story.

The *Squalus* had on board personal lifesaving devices called Momsen lungs, which could be used to escape a sunken ship. However, they had not been tested at a depth of 240 feet and were considered a last resort. A better solution waited two hundred miles away in New London, Connecticut. Navy Commander Charles Momsen, inventor of the Momsen lung, had been testing a rescue chamber he had developed along with Commander Allan McCann, but it had never been used in an actual rescue operation. The decision was made to take Momsen's and McCann's diving bell to the

Squalus. Twenty-three hours after the sub went down, the minesweeper USS *Falcon* was positioned above the stricken sub, carrying the rescue chamber.

After several hours, and not without many glitches, all thirty-three men were rescued. What has been called the "Greatest Submarine Rescue Ever" had been a success. Not long thereafter, the *Squalus* was salvaged and brought to the surface (because of her background in metallurgy and engineering, Malvina Hoffman provided assistance to the navy in the effort). Twenty-five of the deceased men on board were recovered. One man was never found and was presumed to have been lost out of a hatch. The remains of those twenty-five were sent home to the nineteen different states from which they hailed for burial as heroes who gave the ultimate sacrifice in the service of their country.

The *Squalus* was repaired and rechristened the USS *Sailfish* at President Roosevelt's suggestion, and it saw action in World War II. In 1950, Charles "Swede" Momsen designed the USS *Albacore*, the revolutionary design of which greatly increased submarine speed. It is now on display in a fascinating museum in Portsmouth.

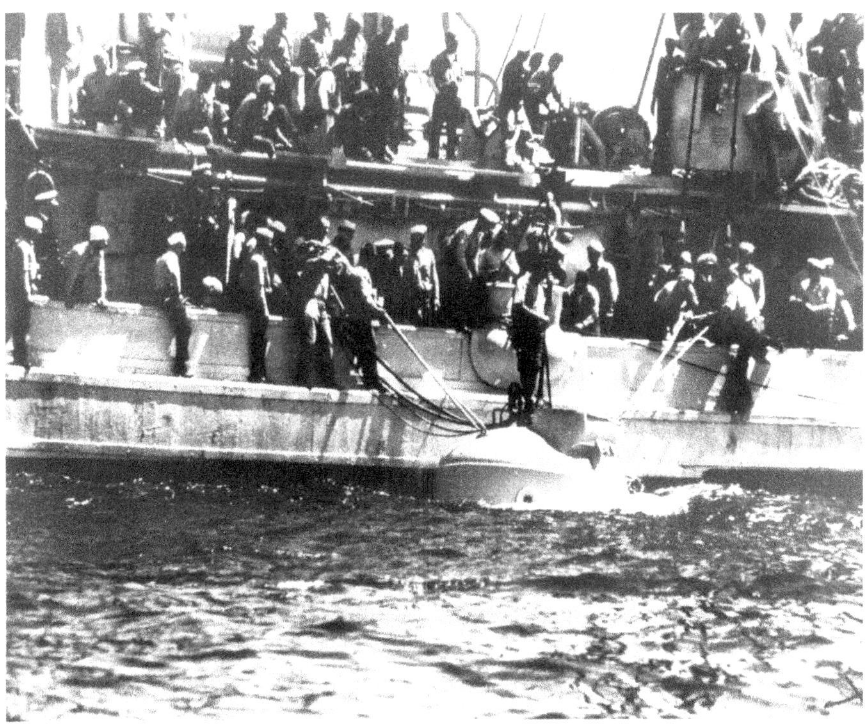

McCann and Momsen's rescue chamber brings the last *Squalus* crewman to safety. *U.S. Navy photo.*

Alice Hobson's memorial and benefit concert featuring the BSO was broadcast coast to coast to a relieved and thankful nation, with survivors of the USS *Squalus* volunteering to serve as ushers. At the end of the concert, "The Star-Spangled Banner" was played. The audience was then invited to congregate on the shore, where a final tribute was paid as a local aviator dropped a wreath on the waters where the *Squalus* went down.

Due to the Depression, many of the summer colony families at Little Boar's Head had to sell their cottages. Colonel George Studebaker's story gives a prime example of the Depression's impact. He was the Studebaker who owned the home on the southern end of Little Boar's Head from 1909 until the 1930s. He had served his country heroically, leading a unit in the Spanish-American War; went on to join the family business and made a fortune in various investments; and then lost it all in the Depression. Batchelder's Hotel burned down in 1929 and was never rebuilt, adding to the demise of the summer colony.

These days, most of the town's residents live there year-round. The fish houses at Little Boar's Head have always been appreciated for their uniqueness and charm. Now, of course, *they* are LBH summer cottages, although not quite on the same scale as those across the road. Next time you're over that way, pull into the North Hampton State Beach parking lot, take a stroll down the King's Highway and reflect on all the stories behind this beautiful place.

The Meetinghouse at Dover Point

Wonderfully preserved is the outline of ancient fortification erected 235 years ago....I know not of another instance in New England where a church was similarly fortified.
—Reverend Dr. George Hall

Preacher Wars

Fish. New Hampshire was founded on fish. There is a Legal Sea Foods ad that says, "Presbyterians will give you a sermon; Pescatarians will give you a salmon." First permanent settler Edward Hilton was not a Presbyterian (he was "C of E"—Church of England), but he most certainly was a pescatarian. Salmon was his business.

Sometime between 1497, when John Cabot explored the northern North American coast on behalf of Henry VII, and 1614, when captain John Smith came by, English sailors began fishing off the New Hampshire coast near the Isles of Shoals. Initially, the good captain thought that it was a good idea to name the islands the "Smith Islands" after himself. In time, they became known by the Isles of Shoals due to "shoaling" or schooling of fish. In the meantime, fishermen would set up temporary camps on the islands, spending the summer fishing and curing the fish to take back home. They even went so far as to set some rules, including one declaring that no women

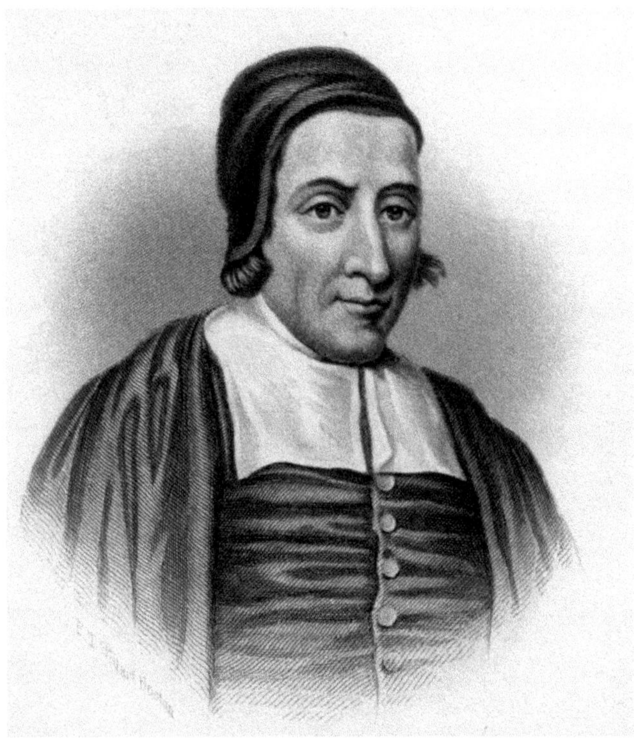

The Reverend Hanserd Knollys, founder of the First Parish Church. *Courtesy of the First Parish Church, Dover.*

were allowed on the islands. When that didn't take, it was, well OK, we'll allow women, but intoxicating beverages can't be sold.

In the spring of 1623, David Thompson settled at Little Harbor, in what is now Odiorne Point in Rye, making him our first recorded settler. But after a few years, he abandoned his settlement and took off to live at the Plymouth Colony in Massachusetts. A little later in 1623, Edward Hilton with two others—his brother William and another man (possibly Thomas Roberts, according to some histories)—along with some laborers, came over to settle at Pomeroy Cove in what is now Dover Point. They stuck around, set about growing their fishing business and built homes and roads. Thus, Dover became New Hampshire's first permanent settlement and therefore America's seventh permanent European settled town. In front are St. Augustine, Florida (1564); Santa Fe, New Mexico (1607); Hampton, Virginia (1610); Albany, New York (1614); Plymouth, Massachusetts (1620); and Weymouth, Massachusetts (1622).

George Wadleigh, in his 1882 history *Notable Events in the History of Dover, New Hampshire*, succinctly lays out the reasons why Hilton, rather than Thompson, chose the right place for starting our state:

> *The whole country was open before them to go in and occupy where they would…and they could hardly have found a more inviting place than the point, either for fishing, planting or trading with the Indians.…For safety no resort could have been better than this narrow neck of land, and from which by their boats there were much immediate means of escape, if escape was at any time necessary. For planting also…so far at least as they could contribute to their own wants, the Pointe was, of all places that which they would select, far preferable to any land near Little Harbor.*

Edward Hilton was born in Cheshire County, England, around 1596. He came from a prosperous family and was well educated. In 1621, he was admitted to the Fishmongers of London guild (now called the Fishmonger's Company), which was a very selective society. Only owners of fishing vessels or wealthy fishing merchants were admitted, so Hilton's admission shows he had high standing in that community. Edward was a good businessman and came well prepared for his settlement, bringing food supplies, livestock, grain for planting and materials for making such things as barrels for transporting fish. And, as hinted at by Wadleigh, he had good relations with the local native people, trading with them and learning their techniques for planting.

In fact, business was the sole reason for Hilton's settlement. As a dedicated member of the Church of England, he did not leave the old country either as a religious dissenter or because of persecution. He was a worshipful man, but he was here to make money. It appears that he went back to England in 1629 and came back not only married but also with a grant, called the Squamscot Grant, giving him all the land on what is now Hilton's Point, widening to encompass the Great Bay and extending three miles inland (the current towns of Stratham, Durham, Dover and parts of Greenland, Newington and Madbury were part of this grant). With his wife he had six children, but unfortunately, her name is unknown—which is very unfair considering it's pretty certain that she had her hands full twenty-four hours a day.

Hilton and his party were the only settlers on Dover Point until 1633, when things started to get really interesting, worship-wise—the Puritans were coming to town. In 1631, Hilton sold his grant to an English Puritan group led by Lords Say and Brooke, who, in turn, employed Thomas Wiggin as their agent in the New World. Wiggin had already been in the area acting as an agent for various settlement groups. In late 1633, he brought around thirty people, mostly Puritans (though some were not as strict as their counterparts in Massachusetts), along with some adherents to the Church of England, to settle on Hilton Point. It was around this time that Edward Hilton pulled up stakes and lived out the rest of his life in Newfields, where he is buried, knowing that fishing was no longer going to be the main activity on Hilton Point.

Wiggin also brought along a man he described as a "worthy Puritan divine," the Reverend William Leveridge, thus beginning the parish on Dover Point. The first service was held there in October 1633, probably in someone's home. It was not long after, certainly no later than 1634, that the first church in Dover was built, the location of which is not precisely known. Despite his good reputation, Reverend Leveridge left for lack of financial support. And as we'll see, that did not turn out so well for the locals.

In 1637, a preacher named Reverend George Burdet came to Dover to fill Leveridge's position. He was a man of intrigue, eventually turning out to be a spy for the Church of England's Archbishop William Laud, who was, in the words of historian Wadleigh, "the most inveterate enemy of the Puritans." Not only did Burdet preach, but he also managed to overthrow Wiggins as the settlement's administrator. He then successfully convinced the townsfolk to install him in that position, thereby making himself the spiritual and political leader of the settlement. About a year later, Captain John Underhill, a leader of the Massachusetts Bay Colony, came to Dover from Boston and convinced the townsfolk—apparently a rather fickle lot—to install himself as the town administrator. At the same time, Underhill gathered a congregation and chose a nonconformist (one who did not adhere to the edicts of the Church of England) named Hanserd Knollys as preacher, thereby setting up a rival church to Reverend Burdet's. Burdet immediately forbade Knollys's preaching. Knollys was an anabaptist—someone who rejects infant baptism and only accepts free will and adult baptism. This belief was anathema to Anglicans and could make someone very unpopular in strict religious circles. In more open-minded New Hampshire, however, he was accepted, even by most Puritans.

Dover Preachers: The Colonial Years of the First Parish Church

William Leveridge (Leverich)	1633–35
George Burdet	1637–38
Hanserd Knollys	1638–41
Thomas Larkham	1640–42

Daniel Maud	1643–55
John Reyner	1655–69
John Reyner Jr.	1669–78
John Pike	1678–1710
Nicholas Sever	1711–15
Jonathon Cushing	1717–69
Jeremy Belknap, DD	1767–86

So, the Dover preacher story so far: William Leveridge leaves because they won't pay him enough even though he got a church built; C of E spy Reverend George Burdet comes in and overthrows the town governor; Anabaptist Hanserd Knollys sets up a rival church but is forbidden to preach by Burdet. Fortunately, the situation seemingly got cleared up in 1638 when Captain Underhill convinced the townsfolk to accept Knollys as their minister. Then, according to Wadleigh's history:

> *The disreputable character of Burdet soon manifested itself and he left Dover and went to Agamenticus, now York, Maine, where his reputation followed him and his career was but a repetition of the practices of which he had been guilty in Dover. He was indicted for adultery and fined twenty pounds sterling, on repeated occasions.*

Acting wisely for a change, Burdet scurried from New England and lived out his days back in England.

Meanwhile, it was under Reverend Knollys's leadership that in 1638 the First Parish Church of Dover was formally organized; it is still going strong after more than 380 years. At this point, with strange Burdet gone and the parish church firmly established, one might think that everyone lived happily ever after, ecclesiastically speaking. But then along came Thomas Larkham. Larkham had been a minister at Northam, Dorsetshire, in his native England. Considered to be a radical preacher, he was charged with heresy, treason and witchcraft in King Charles I's anti-Puritan Court of the Star Chamber, so after inheriting some money, he figured the time might be right to head to New England. He came to Massachusetts around 1640 but found the strict religious discipline there not to his liking, so he came up to Dover. Dr. Jeremy Belknap (#11 on the preacher list) wrote of him, "The people of Dover were much taken with his preaching....Not being able to retain two ministers, they resolved to cast out Mr. Knolles [*sic*] and embrace Mr. Larkham." Bowing to the popular will, Knollys gracefully withdrew from his position as minister. Before long, Reverend Larkham started upsetting people by taking into the church all persons who wanted to join, even those "notoriously immoral or ignorant, if they would but promise amendment" (which, as anyone who attended Sunday school would think, seems like a good thing). Anyway, while he was at it, he appointed himself town governor and, just for good measure, renamed the town Northam after his parish in Dorset.

All this was too much for Reverend Knollys. As Dr. Belknap wrote, "The more religious sort still adhering to Mr. Knolles, he, in their name, excommunicated Mr. Larkham, who in turn, laid violent hands on Mr. Knolles, taking his hat from his head, pretending it was not paid for; but he was so civil as to send it to him again." All's well that ends well, right? After all, both of these ministers happened to be fellow Cambridge men.

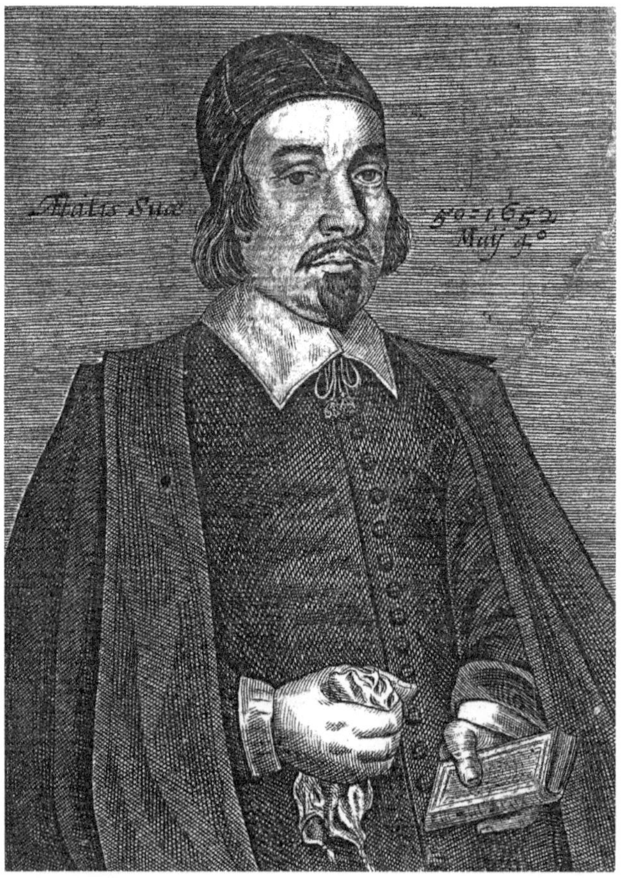

The Reverend Thomas Larkham, Reverend Knollys's rival. *Courtesy of the Tavistock United Reformed Church, Devonshire, UK.*

Apparently not. Reverend Larkham, as governor, gathered some magistrates and assembled a company to bring Captain Underhill, Reverend Knollys's sponsor, to court. Underhill, carrying a Bible attached to a halberd (a fearsome weapon that is a combination of pike and battle axe—perfect for displaying the Good Book) as a sort of banner, gathered some of his own supporters to defend themselves and set out to confront Larkham's group. Reverend Knollys, carrying a pistol (!), joined Underhill's group. Apparently, both of these men of God forgot to wear their WWJD bracelets that day. Reverend Larkham, seeing that he was outgunned (one to zero), wisely beat retreat and sent for Governor Francis Williams of Strawberry Bank (now Portsmouth). Williams came up with a company of armed men and held Captain Underhill and his followers until a court could be held. Williams, acting as judge, found Underhill and the others "guilty of a riot," assessed a fine of one hundred pounds (a lot of dough back then; a good carpenter might make twenty pounds per year) to each of them and banished them from the colony. A petition was sent to the Massachusetts Bay Colony to intervene in the dispute, and the governor sent emissaries to get to the bottom of things. Both sides were found to be at fault, so Knollys revoked Larkham's excommunication and Larkham's side revoked the fines and banishment. So in the end, everyone did live happily ever after.

Here, then, is the Dover preacher final recap: William Leveridge leaves because they won't pay him enough; C of E spy George Burdet comes in and overthrows the town governor; Anabaptist Hanserd Knollys sets up a rival church but is forbidden to preach by Burdet; Knollys wins out because everyone gets tired of Burdet's shenanigans, and then he founds the first church in Dover; Reverend Larkham comes to town, and the townsfolk fire Knollys as minister because they think Larkham is a better preacher; Larkham then upsets half the town by being too nice to people who actually could use some saving, and also he appoints himself town boss and changes the town name to Northam; Knollys excommunicates Larkham over these outrages and gets his hat knocked off and taken (but he gets it back); everything almost comes to blows but doesn't because Knollys is packing heat; Knollys's side gets found guilty of rioting; finally the governor of the Massachusetts Bay Colony steps in and orders everyone to stop behaving like idiots, which they all agree to do. And all this happened in the first nine years of worship in Dover (aka Northam).

A story in an 1875 commemorative newspaper called *Old Dover*, written by Robert Welch, summed up these disputes very neatly. There were two

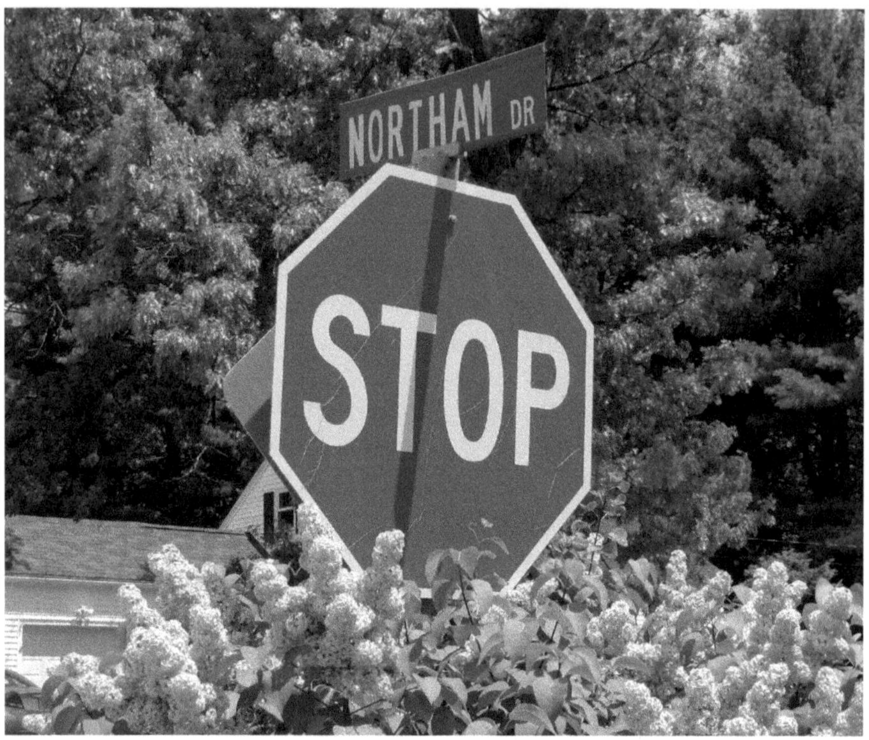

The last remnant of Northam town, on the corner of Maplewood, Dover. *Author's photo.*

factions in Dover, just as there were in England at the time—those loyal to the king and Church of England and those supporting the Parliamentarians and free, independent religions such as the Puritans—and they often fought each other for control of the town. Back in England, these differences led to civil war and the temporary overthrow of the monarchy.

Thankfully, Dover's fifth minister, Daniel Maud, followed the tumultuous period from 1633 to 1642 with some much-needed sanity. Dr. Belknap says of him: "He was an honest man, and of a quiet and peaceable disposition, qualities much wanted in all his predecessors." With his wife, Mary, he instituted the first school in Dover from his home. Finally, the parish members could begin to go about the work of earnestly building their church. By 1642, both Hanserd Knollys and Thomas Larkham had ended their ministries in Dover and gone back to live in England.

Reverend Knollys turns out to have been sort of a religious star during his lifetime. His time in Dover was a relatively short but significant stopping point in his career. Ordained in the Church of England in

1629, Knollys soon began to doubt the tenets of the church and resigned his ministry soon thereafter. This made things rather uncomfortable for him in England, which is why he made it to the New World, and Dover, in 1638. Upon his return to England, he became outspoken in his beliefs that it should not be illegal to fail to adhere to the teachings of the Church of England, and he was frequently jailed throughout his long life for refusing to be silent—including serving six months when he was eighty-six. In 1645, he founded one of the first Baptist churches in London and is considered to be among the most influential of the early Baptists. Knollys supported the Parliamentarians in the English Civil War, serving for a time as their army chaplain. After the restoration of the monarchy in 1660, he was imprisoned (again!) for several weeks until pardoned by Charles II upon his coronation. In addition to preaching, he also worked as an educator and published some sixteen books, including grammars in Latin, Hebrew and Greek, as well as religious subjects and an autobiography. Reverend Knollys died in 1692 at the age of ninety-three. So, in addition to founding one of the very first churches in New Hampshire, Knollys, even though during his time in Dover he considered himself to be a Puritan, turned out to be in the company of some of the first Baptist ministers in the entire New World.

George Wadleigh's book not only provides an in-depth historical account of the founding of Dover but also includes many vignettes from early records, providing a glimpse into everyday life. Most of them are from court proceedings, but some are from contemporary personal diaries. Here are a few examples; more will be sprinkled in as time goes by:

> *6th mo. 31* [1643]—*George Webb was presented by the Court for living idle like a swine.* [No word on the penalty for swine-like living.]
> *Sept. 27* [1648]—*It was ordered that all such person or persons that shall be found absent without lawful cause from the town meeting shall for such default pay a fine of six shillings.*

Also on that day:

> *It was ordered that Richard Pinkham shall beat the drum on Lord's day to give notice for the time of meeting.* [If Mr. Pinkham's drum beating didn't get you to the meeting, you certainly deserved the fine.]

The court proceedings on July 9, 1651, cleared up a lot of unseemly behavior:

> *George Walton was presented for abusing the Lord's day in carrying boards and going to the Isle of Shoals. Admonished.*
> *Philip Chesley, Thomas Footman, Thomas Johnson and William Roberts presented for going in the time of meeting to the ordinary* [tavern] *on the afternoon of the 25th May last. Admonished.*
> *Thomas Footman was presented for abusing the constable, Thomas Beard, and fined 13s. 4 d.* [13 shillings and 4 pence—around two-thirds of a pound].

A word of explanation about those dates. First, until England and its colonies adopted the Gregorian calendar in 1752, the new year officially began on March 25, the day of the Feast of the Annunciation—also known as Lady Day. Second, in Quaker-style dating, the months were numbered rather than named due to the fact that Quakers disapproved of the pagan origin of the names of the first eight months of the year. This made March the first month of the year—not too big a deal when spelling out the months but pretty confusing when the Quaker style was used, as it was from time to time. Therefore, the date of the first vignette above ("6th mo. 31") actually means August 31, since August is the sixth month of the year counting from March.

It gets even more confusing around the March 25 New Year: "1 mo. 10" (March 10), **1645**, for example, would in reality be only twenty days before "1 mo. 30" (March 30), **1646**, since the year had just changed on March 25. Sometimes folks at the time might write "1 mo. 10, 1645/46" to try and keep things straight, but since it wasn't consistently done, confusion could reign pretty easily. Just to add to the fun, most other countries went to the Gregorian calendar in 1582. This meant, for example, that in France when it was January 1, 1645, the same day in England was January 1, 1644, because 1645 did not start until March. Historians try to avoid the confusion by calling pre-Gregorian dates "Old Style" (OS), and dates after that are called "New Style" (NS).

A MIGHTY FORTRESS IS OUR CHURCH

It was during Reverend Maud's tenure that the second meetinghouse was built. From the town records:

> *5, 10th. mo: 1652 (O.S.)—Mr. Richard Walderne...doth bind himself... to erect a meeting house on the hill near Elder Nutter's; the dementions of said house is to be forty foot longe; twenty six foot wide, sixteen foot stud, with six windows, two doors...and to plancke all the walls; with glass and nails for it; and to be finished betwixt this and April next, come twelve months, wch will be in the year 1654.*

There are no spelling mistakes here; the writer of this record seemed to abbreviate when he felt like it, and Mr. Webster was not to come along for another 150 years. Mr. Walderne brought in the new building on time, in exchange for which he received rights to build a mill. A dedication was held in April 1654. There still being no bell, Richard Pinkham dutifully beat his drum to call everyone to the joyous event. Four years later, the townsfolk voted in favor of some upgrades to the new meeting house, including "a pulpet and seats Conveniente to be made, & a Bell to be purchased," and so Mr. Pinkham's drum was finally retired. On June 25, 1667, there was

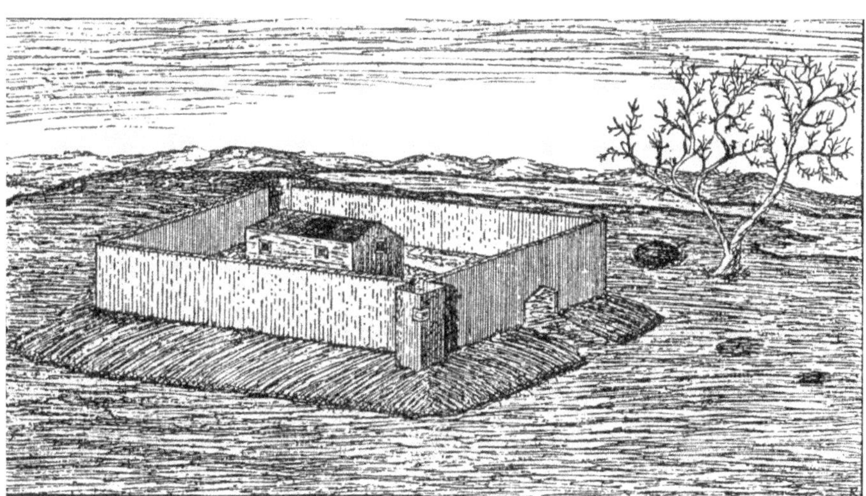

This drawing is the only image of the only known meetinghouse with a fort around it in the United States. Dover Point Road is not shown; it would have been to the immediate right of the structure running north toward the upper right corner of the drawing. *From* Notable Events in the History of Dover New Hampshire, *1882*.

some very good news indeed from the town council: "Goodman Kirke of Dover. Licensed to keep a house of entertainment." Then, a few days later, the event that prompted this chapter: "By ye sellecktmen ye 4th. 5th Mo: 67 (O.S.)—It is Agried with Capt. Coffin to Buld the forte about the metting house on Dover Neck, one hundred foot square with two Sconces of sixteen foot square, and all the timber to be twelve inches thick and the wall to be eight foot high, with sells and Braces."

A lot of meetinghouses in New England were fortified in that the buildings themselves were strengthened to protect against attacks by Native Americans. The second Dover meetinghouse is the only known example of one in which a palisade was built surrounding it, complete with "sconces," or watch towers. The immediate rationale to build these defenses is not clear because at that time there were no instances of hostilities between the Native Americans and the local settlers.

Over 350 years later, the foundations of the palisades are still visible. The fact that these foundations are still largely intact today has provoked wonder over the generations. In 1877, New Hampshire historian (and Civil War veteran, Massachusetts Board of Education member, New Hampshire legislature member and pastor to many congregations) Dr. Alonzo Quint commented, "The rains of two hundred and ten years have not been able to wash away the earthwork which the fathers built around their small house of worship."

In 1902, First Parish Church minister Dr. George Hall wrote, "Wonderfully preserved is the outline of ancient fortification erected 235 years ago….I know not of another instance in New England where a church was similarly fortified."

And in a 1983 historical survey commissioned by the church, David Bryant and David Starbuck marvel at the foundation remains: "The site remains today practically the only visible and well-preserved reminder of the town's early history. Rarely has any 17th century site, meeting house or otherwise, been preserved so carefully and faithfully to this very day."

The construction of the fortress walls was known to be finished by 1675. Although the fort was planned to be 100 feet on a side, the diagram provided in the National Register of Historic Places form shows the main embankment to be about 96.5 feet long by 79 to 80 feet wide, but when you add in the sconces, the dimensions come pretty close to the original plan. The actual dimensions of the meetinghouse, planned to be 40 by 26 feet, are not known. The answer to that mystery will likely come from archaeology. The authors of the National Register of Historic Places Nomination Form, Donald Bryant and David Starbuck, conclude their report stating, "Historic

THE
GRANITE MONTHLY.

A MAGAZINE OF LITERATURE, HISTORY AND STATE PROGRESS.

VOL. I. NOVEMBER, 1877. NO. 7.

THE FIRST CHURCH IN DOVER, AND ITS PASTOR.

BY ALONZO H. QUINT, D. D.

THE YEAR 1667.

If one will take the old Neck road at Pine Hill cemetery in Dover; go past the Wingate farm on which the Wingates, six generations of them, have lived continuously since the year 1662; cross Little John's creek; follow the road up Huckleberry Hill, and continue a mile or so on the elevated plateau beyond, he will see, on his right, and touching the road at a point where the road begins to descend decidedly, the well marked remnants of an earth-work. The work is perfectly traceable; the only loss being at one corner of the southeastern projection for sentries, which is on the roadside, and where some vandal of a road-surveyor cut away a small portion for the sake of gravel. That earth was once crowned with a strong palisade, and within it stood the second meeting house of "The First Church in Dover." The rains of two hundred and ten years have not been able to wash away the earth-work which the fathers built around their small house of worship. "Forty foot longe, twenty-six foot wide, sixteen foot stud," was that meeting house; with six windows, two doors, tile covering, and "with glass and nails for it." It was in 1653 that that second edifice was built. On that house they placed a turret in 1665, and in it, from that year, swung the bell they bought in England; before which time, from 1648, Richard Pinkham, by town authority, had summoned the people to church by beat of his drum.

It was in 1667 they built the "fort," as the old records called it, for a defence against the Indians. The ground slopes rapidly on each side of the work. The palisade was one hundred feet square, with "two sconces of sixteen foot square." The timbers were twelve inches thick, and the wall eight feet high, with sills and braces. Inside the inclosure the men stacked their arms on the Lord's day; and inside the two "sconces," which stood on alternate corners, the sentinels watched. They could see far up and down the road north and

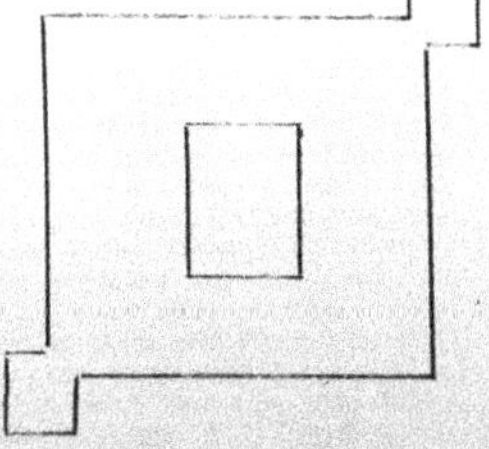

Left: The November 1877 issue of the *Granite Monthly* with Dr. Quint's diagram of the fortified meetinghouse's earthworks. *Courtesy of the Dover Public Library.*

Below: The First Parish Church sign on Dover Point Road showing the southeast sconce foundations and the DAR's protective wall (keeping erosion at bay) with 1902 plaque. *Author's photo.*

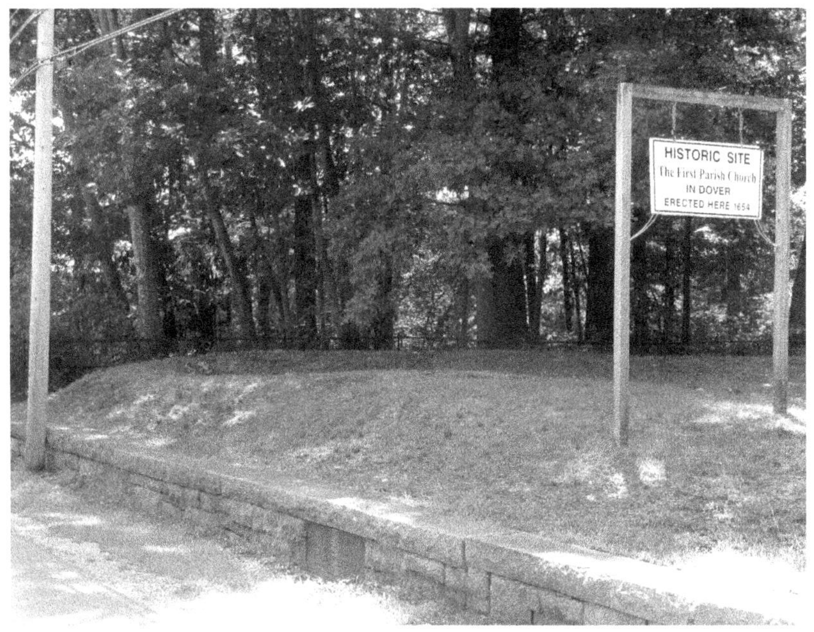

archeology has the potential for testing the accuracy of available historical documentation, for getting the real dimensions of the meeting house and palisades, and for revealing numerous construction details of one of the oldest meeting houses in New Hampshire."

As Quint, Hall, Bryant and Starbuck all observed, the site is indeed still well preserved. This is especially surprising given that the current First Parish Church, a few miles up the road near downtown Dover, is not anywhere near this land and that there has been a lot of development around it over the years. Dover Point Road is also a very busy road, providing a direct connection to Newington and Portsmouth, with a high school, many neighborhoods and a large working farm with a popular marketplace along the way. The first clue that there is something significant to see on the site is that the sign placed by the church to mark the site has one leg shorter than the other—the reason being, of course, that it is standing on a mound of the earthworks. The sign reads:

Historic Site
The First Parish Church
In Dover
Erected Here 1654

The sign itself is a bit confusing as this is actually the site of the second meetinghouse, the long-disappeared first meetinghouse being a short distance away. Stopping to view the site, it really is a marvel to see the complete foundations of the stockade after all those centuries. The retaining wall along the roadside, complete with plaque, was installed in 1902 by—once again—the Daughters of the American Revolution. This time, the Margery Sullivan Chapter, which serves Dover, Durham, Rollinsford and Somersworth, did the good works. The regent at the time was Fannie Dow French, who, perhaps not all that surprisingly, was a descendent of General Joseph Cilley. In 1907, the Margery Sullivan Chapter added an iron fence surrounding the three sides away from the road to further enhance and protect the site.

The photos show the remains of the northwest and southeast sections of the fortress wall, including sconces, in correspondence with the 1983 archaeological plan. The position of the sconces can be seen by the depressions in the embankment corners. The DAR-installed fences can be seen in the background.

Meanwhile, back in town, some jurisprudence, per Wadleigh:

October 15, 1659—With a due regard for the proprieties of life the authorities convicted...the following persons of not going to meeting: William Roberts of Oyster River, who had been absent 28 Sundays. William Follett, 16 days [absent from meeting]. *James Smith, 14 days* [absent] *and one day "confest" to have been at a Quaker meeting, for which he was fined 10 shillings. Thomas Roberts, 13 days* [absent]. *James Nute, sen.* [Sr.] *and wife and son. 26 days* [absent] *and for entertaining Quakers 4 hours in one day...fined 40 shillings an hour according to the law.* [Doing some math here—the Nute family total fine was 160 shillings, or 8 pounds sterling. According to a conversion chart provided by Eric Nye of the University of Wyoming, that would be a little over $1,500 today. That was one expensive party.]

September 15, 1667—The town grand jury presented the town for want of stocks, whipping post, standard weights and measures, a sealer of leather, a pound, a watch house, powder match and bullets. The court enjoined the town to provide themselves with these accompaniments of civilization... or pay a fine of 5 pounds and 2s, 6d fees. [Not sure that "whipping post" belongs on a list of "accompaniments of civilization."]

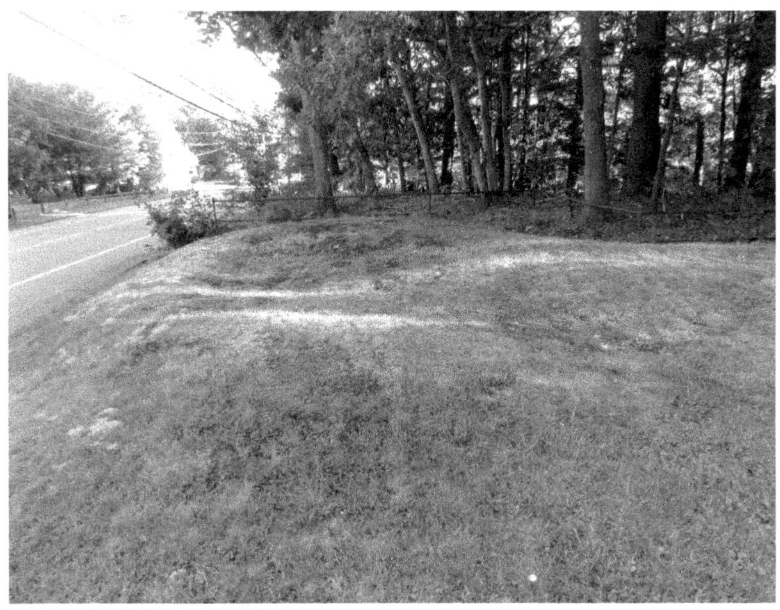

The east fortification earthworks, with southeast sconce foundation. *Author's photo.*

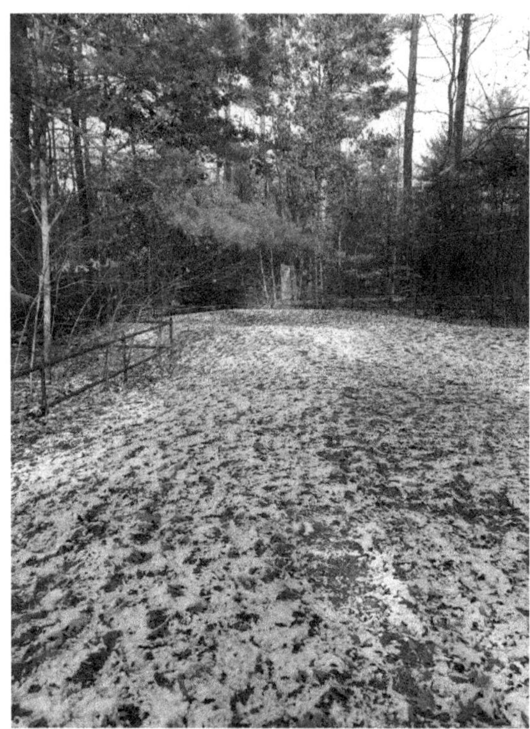

Left: The west meetinghouse fortification earthworks, with northwest sconce foundation. *Author's photo.*

Below: The church fortification earthworks archaeological diagram. North is at the top. The photo of the west side earthworks with sconce lines up directly with the drawing. The east side earthworks with sconce photo is at 180 degrees of the drawing. *From the National Register of Historic Places Inventory, Nomination Form, 1983.*

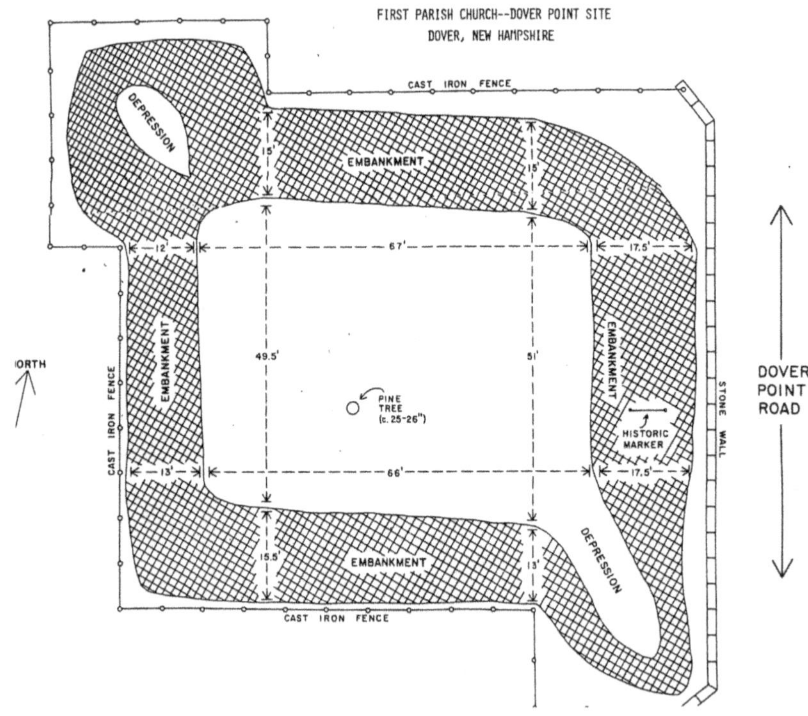

> *July 14, 1668—Ordered by the selectman that forthwith the Constable shall take of William Williams, sen. by way of distress the sum of 19 shillings for a fine for a breach of a town order for entertaining Naomi Hull.* [There's a fine for entertaining Naomi?]

Whatever the rationale was for the 1667 decision to build the walls around the meetinghouse, by 1675, a very real need arose. In alliance with the French, local Native Americans began what turned out to be fifty years of hostilities against the settlers begun by Wahowah, a local sagamore (chief), acting on a plea from his people that the settlers had stolen their land. Dr. Quint's article states, "Inside the enclosure men stacked their arms on the Lord's Day; and inside the two 'sconces,' which stood on alternate corners, the sentinels watched."

The threat of attack was so concerning that several nearby homes were built as "garrisons," which gave Dover its nickname as the "Garrison City." Typically, garrison houses are built with defense in mind: firing ports from a second-story overhang; thick log walls; small windows; a portcullis (a heavy door that slides down from above). One of the oldest houses in New Hampshire is the 1675 William Damm garrison, moved in 1916 from its original site off Back River Road to the Woodman Museum near downtown Dover. The fact that these hostilities lasted for such a long period kept Dover's growth slow, as few new settlers would want to bring their families to such a dangerous place. As it turned out, however, the area of Dover Neck around the meetinghouse never was involved in the hostilities with the local Native Americans.

THE KINDNESS OF STRANGERS

Meanwhile, more religious conflicts, frankly of a more serious nature, were going on. For some reasons, a lot of Puritans had a big problem with peace-loving, independent-minded folks, i.e., Quakers. Dr. Quint explained it well: "The liberty of American Puritanism in its early days was liberty for itself to do what it determined, but liberty for nobody else."

Puritanism helped provide a stable, safe society, but it did have its excesses. Perhaps nowhere else was this so apparent than in Dover. Exhibit A: James Nute's 160-shilling fine for entertaining Quakers that afternoon in 1659.

Exhibit B is a lot worse. In 1642, Dover voted, not without some dissent, to become part of Massachusetts, a circumstance that would last until 1679. Joining Massachusetts of course meant that Dover was subject to Massachusetts laws, including laws against Quakers. Missionaries were often sent to New England by the Quakers, who would challenge the established church authority—preaching against professional ministers and Puritan restrictions on individual conscience, for example, and generally upsetting the apple cart of church-run communities. To make matters worse, they would, among other things, travel on the Sabbath, preach in the market place and refuse to take off their hats in the presence of officials. As a result, persecution of Quakers was widespread on both sides of the Atlantic. Banishment from town was the usual penalty for such behavior, but in 1661, a law was passed calling for Quakers to be driven from town or even from the entire Massachusetts Bay Colony jurisdiction using extremely cruel methods (this being a family book, the details of those methods will be left out). In 1662, three Quaker women from England, Ann Coleman, Mary Tompkins and Alice Ambrose, arrived in Dover and began to hold meetings and services around town—including debating Puritan minister John Reyner. After several weeks, some town elders decided that enough was enough, so on December 22, 1662, the local Crown magistrate, Richard Walderne (the same guy who built the second church), issued the following order:

> *To the constables of Dover, Hampton, Salisbury, Newbury, Rowley, Ipswich, Wenham, Lynn, Boston, Roxbury, Dedham, and until these vagabond Quakers* [the three women] *are carried out of this jurisdiction. You, and every one of you, are required, in the King's Majesty's name, to take these vagabond Quakers…and make them fast to a cart's tail, and driving the cart through your several towns…* [inflict severe physical punishment on them] *in each town; and so to convey them from constable to constable till they are out of this jurisdiction.*

The plan was to carry out the sentence on the women through each town all the way to Rhode Island. Fortunately, the constable in Salisbury, Massachusetts, refused to carry out the order, and he allowed a local man, Dr. Walter Barefoot, to take the three to safety in Maine. Ironically, the women eventually returned to Dover (given what they endured, a very brave act) and helped found the Dover Quaker congregation. Not too many years later, one-third of Dover residents were Quakers. Meanwhile, in 1883, John Greenleaf Whittier, himself a Quaker (and after whom the I-95 bridge over

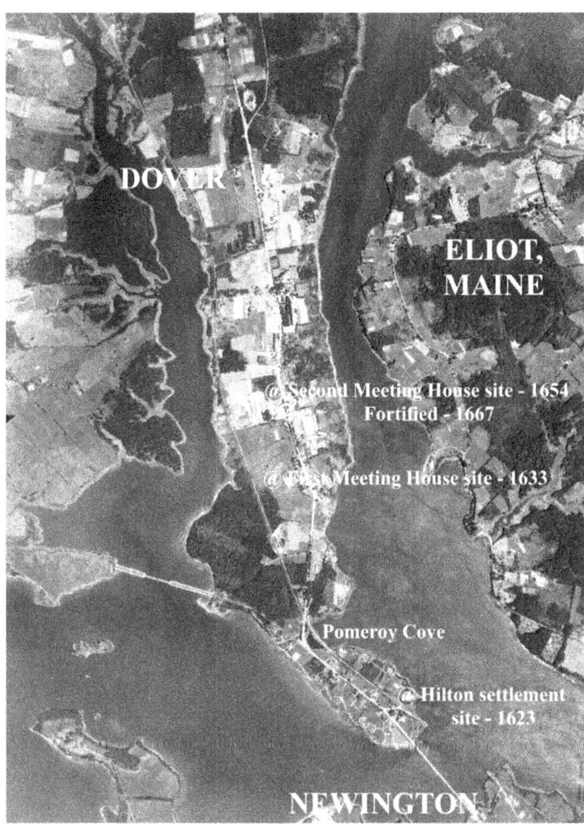

Dover Point, pre–Spaulding Turnpike, showing key early sites. U.S. War Department photo, 1940. *Courtesy of the Strafford County Conservation District.*

the Merrimack River in Amesbury is named), penned a poignant poem called "How the Women Went from Dover," immortalizing the women and their sad story. Not surprisingly, Richard Walderne did not come out looking so good in Whittier's poem. The Dover Quaker Meeting House has on display a sobering painting memorializing the event. Built in 1768, it is the oldest church building in town.

As the years went by, the population center of Dover moved north from Dover Neck up into the village of Cocheco, in the area of the present Dover town center. Of course, this led to—what else?—more conflict. Thankfully, of a more peaceable type. In 1713, the residents of Cocheco built a meetinghouse by private subscription rather than by town order (church house number three, if you're keeping count). With just one minister in town, there was obviously an issue of where the minister would preach on the Sabbath. All the while, daily life goes on. More from Wadleigh's book, many of these courtesy of Reverend John Pike's diary:

November 8, 1684—Was exceeding dark, from 10 in the morning, till two in the afternoon, which might be occasioned by a very black and thick dark cloud, passing over very low. It seemed as though the sun had been greatly and totally eclipsed. [According to NASA, there was no solar eclipse anywhere that day or any other day close by.]

December 25, 1692—A woeful and tremendous noise was affirmed to be heard in the air nigh Cap't Gerrish's garrison, which continued with a little intermission for half an hour. [Pike]

October 15, 1693—Sabbath day, about 10 o'clock in the morning, a great rumbling sound was heard by many towards the northeast, supposed to be a considerable earthquake. [Pike]

October 19, 1698—A violent northeast storm of rain, which melting the [recent] *snows caused an extraordinary freshet, flowing higher than the observation of the oldest standers in these parts—carried away many logs and boards, and endangered the very mills.* [Pike]

January 31, 1699—A considerable earthquake happened about 1 o'clock this day, and another the night following, if it was not a clap of thunder.

September 6, 1700—Travelling in Amesbury woods with two more in my company, we killed a rattlesnake near Hunt's new field, which had three rattles on ye end of its tail, with which he made a prodigious and terrible noise. [Pike]

January 15, 1704—Happened the highest tide ever was observed in these parts of the country. Did great damage to warehouses and cellars; carried away some houses and many stages at the Isles of Shoals; transported many haystacks, and in some places tore up great quantities of marsh and removed it far off into other places. [Pike]

December 24, 1716—The "multiplicity of public houses occasioning many disorders," the assembly enacted that there be but six taverns in Portsmouth, three in Hampton, two in Dover, one at Oyster River, two at Exeter, two at New Castle, and one in the parish of Newington, and that "all other tippling house be suppressed." [As always, Portsmouth has all the fun.]

> *March 7, 1718* [from the *Boston News Letter*]—*We are informed from Dover that snow lies two feet deep on the ground, and that several parts are bare on the Neck, where last week were seen swarms of grasshoppers, some hopping and some flying, which considering the season of the year and the nature of the creatures seems very strange.*

And so there you have it: storms, earthquakes, floods, pestilence, darkness at noon, limits on pubs—the settlers of our state were a hearty breed indeed. Frankly, it's a miracle anybody is here at all.

At a town meeting on August 17, three townsmen requested that the issue of which church should be the main worship site be discussed at the next General Assembly meeting. In May 1714, it was voted that while town business meetings would still be held at the old church on Dover Neck, the worship should alternate weekly between the two churches. A study committee was formed to try to bring some resolution to the issue, but it was unable to do so. With the population in Cocheco outstripping that of Dover Neck, the parish council finally decided in 1720 to move all church services to Cocheco "except one Sabbath or two" at Dover Neck. Well, everyone knows what vague language like that means. By 1725, services were no longer held on Dover Point. In 1758, a fourth meetinghouse was erected, this time on the site of the present meetinghouse of the First Parish Congregational Church, built in 1829. At some point, the old meetinghouse grounds reverted to private hands. In 1880, two church members—former governor Jonathon Sawyer and Elisha Brown—reacquired the land and deeded it to the church in perpetuity with the stipulation that it shall be "improved, marked and utilized in such a manner as will preserve and perpetuate its historical associations as the 'The Old Meeting House Lot.'"

So, thanks to some outstanding building skills by Dover's early settlers and the careful stewardship over the years by the church, the generous land donors and the DAR, those three-and-a-half-century-old mounds can still be visited, admired and contemplated.

Broth Hill, the City of Seth

We must destroy slavery, or it will destroy liberty.
—Henry Wilson

From Manchester to Rollinsford and from Nashua to Berlin, manufacturers needed to provide accommodations, preferably close to the work site, for the large numbers of employees they needed to work the factories. Much of this housing, from tenements to row houses to supervisors' homes, is still in everyday use and can be easily spotted. On the other hand, sometimes workers' housing is not typical and can be hidden in plain sight.

In our state, sometimes just going from point A to point B provides a great drive. One such journey is Route 108 between Exeter and Dover. Traveling south from Dover, the road passes through the charming, revitalized town center of Newmarket, skirts just east of pristine Newfields village (where Edward Hilton is buried) and then carries on through Durham. A short distance south of Durham's town hall, there are five surprisingly similar houses situated on the east side of the road, set next to one another just past the town pound. Observing closely, they appear to be part of a planned development—except that while the three southernmost homes are largely identical, the two northern ones are somewhat more elaborate. At the same time, all five seem to share similar footprints. The first clue to what they were all about comes from that indispensable historian's friend: Zillow. One of those five houses was recently listed for sale on that real estate site. After

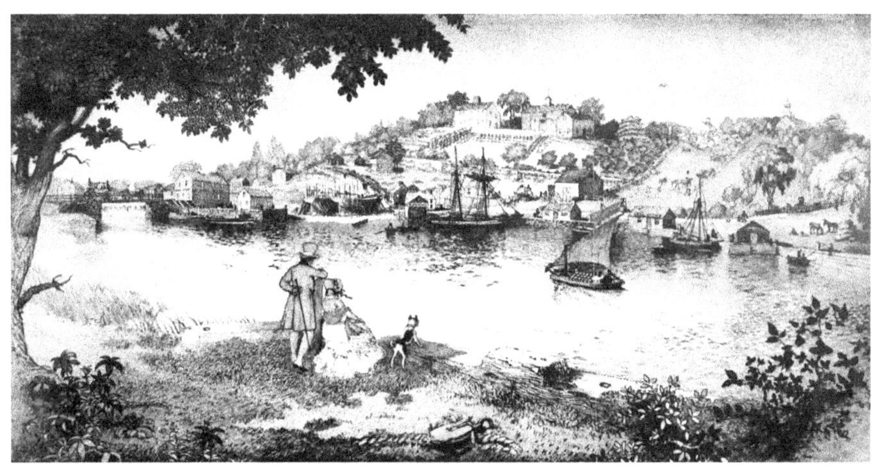

An 1825 view of the Oyster River from Sullivan's Wharf. Shipbuilding activity, such as might have been done by Joseph Coe, can be seen underway across the river. *From* History of the Town of Durham, *1913; courtesy of the Dover Public Library.*

describing the home's "stunning wood floor" and "dining room accented with original exposed wood beams," it included this very useful bit of information: located on "historical Broth Hill." Mary P. Thompson, in her 1892 *Landmarks of Ancient Dover* (bearing in mind that Durham was once a part of Dover), explains:

> *Broth Hill…is a well-known height at the south end of Durham village, commanding a beautiful view of the Oyster river valley and the hilly, winding village beyond, in its most picturesque aspect.…There is a story that this name was given in derision of the favorite dish of the workmen once employed in the Durham ship-yards, for whom several cottages had been built on this height.*

In reality, Thompson explains that the name "Broth Hill" appears to be derived from the Coolbroth (sometimes spelled Colbath or Colbroath) family, who lived there in the eighteenth century. New Hampshire's only vice president, Henry Wilson, was of that family. In fact, at his birth in Farmington, New Hampshire, in 1812, he was named Jeremiah Jones Colbath. As described by the late senator Mark O. Hatfield of Oregon in his 1997 book about U.S. vice presidents, Henry Wilson's life "was like a Dickens novel. Like Pip, David Copperfield, and Nicholas Nickleby, he overcame a childhood of hardship and privation through the strength of his character, his ambition, and occasional assistance from others." His rather

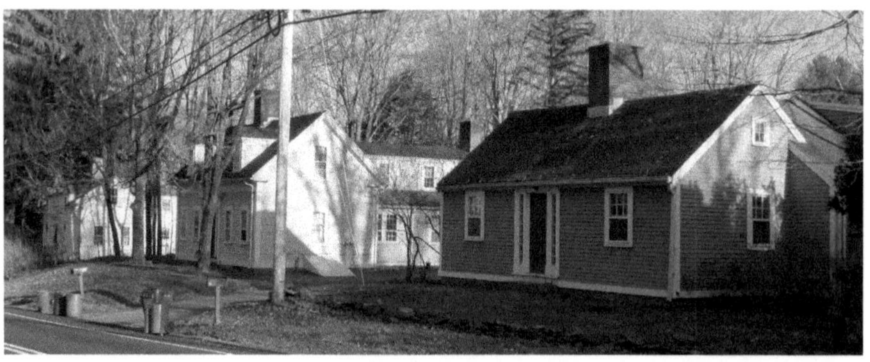

Three shipwrights' cottages built circa 1800 by shipbuilder Joseph Coe. *Author's photo.*

lazy and out-of-control father named him after a wealthy neighbor in hopes that this would somehow induce the gentleman to leave an inheritance to the family. Not surprisingly, this did not pan out. Instead, the Colbaths "lived hand to mouth." According to Senator Hatfield's biography, Henry Wilson would later say, "I know what it is to ask a mother for bread when she had none to give."

Because of his father's ridiculous plan, young Jeremiah hated his name so much that he changed it as soon as he came of age. Senator Hatfield goes on to say that Wilson's new choice of name was inspired by either a Philadelphia teacher whose biography he had read or that of an English preacher whose painting he had seen; no one seems to know for sure. At the age of ten, his father arranged an apprenticeship for him that would bind him until he turned twenty-one. This arrangement made any formal schooling nearly impossible, so instead, Henry began to read every book—history, philosophy, biography—that he could get his hands on. In 1833, now twenty-one and released from his indenture, Henry looked for work in the New Hampshire mills, but finding none, he walked the one hundred miles from Farmington to Boston, eventually settling a few miles west in Natick. There, he learned shoemaking from a friend and became quite successful, eventually opening his own factory.

In 1836, Henry visited Washington, D.C., and while there, he witnessed slaves working in the fields of Virginia and Maryland as well as slave pens and auctions in view of the Capitol building. According to Senator Hatfield, he went home determined "to give all that I had…to the cause of emancipation in America." Later on he stated, "We must destroy slavery, or it will destroy liberty." Wilson joined the Whig Party, and in 1840, he was elected to the Massachusetts House of Representatives, serving several terms before being elected to the Massachusetts Senate, where he also served several terms. He became disillusioned with proslavery factions within the Whig Party and converted to the Free-Soilers before joining the new, strongly antislavery Republicans. In 1855, he was elected to a vacant Massachusetts U.S. Senate seat, which he held until his election to vice president as President Ulysses S. Grant's running mate in 1872. He died in office in 1875 at the age of sixty-three. One of Henry Wilson's proudest achievements was introducing the bill in Congress that outlawed slavery in the District of Columbia. Senator Hatfield, in his book, summed up Wilson's life this way: "He did not simply follow the winds of public opinion whichever way they blew. Throughout his long political career, Wilson remained remarkably consistent in his support for human freedom and equality of rights for all men and women regardless of their color or class." All in all, quite a remarkable life for young Jeremiah Jones Colbath of Farmington, New Hampshire.

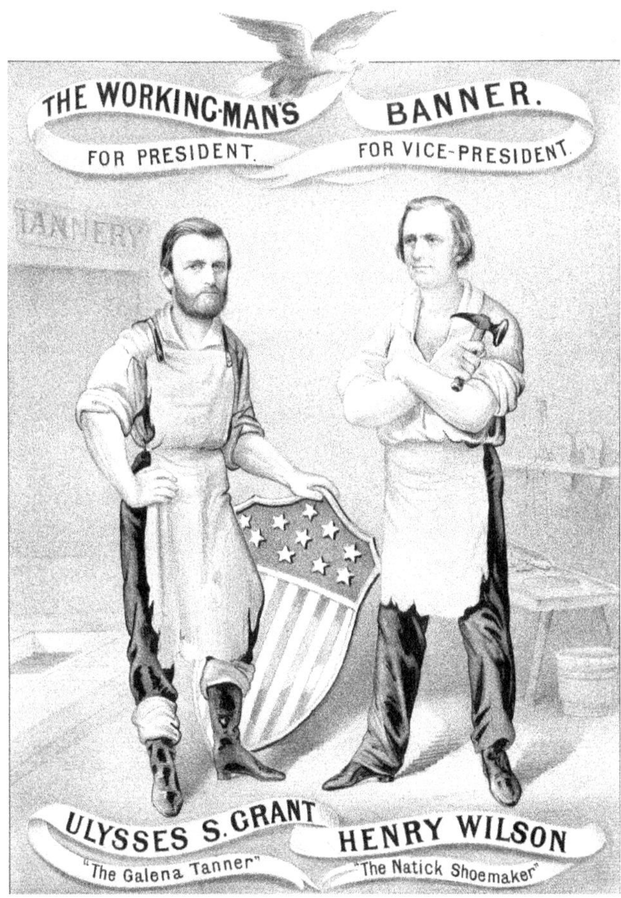

An 1872 Republican Party campaign poster featuring Ulysses S. Grant and New Hampshire–born Henry Wilson. *Library of Congress photo.*

A rather enigmatic rhyme concerning Broth Hill, also reported by Mary P. Thompson, goes like this:

Broth Hill, the city of Seth;
Were it not for Joe Coe,
They would all starve to death.

"Seth" appears to be one Seth Walker, who became proprietor of a public house nearby in 1686 when he married Sarah Smith, the owner's daughter. (Why the Broth Hill area is also known as the city of Seth can only be due to a grateful appreciation for a good pub!) Joseph "Joe" Coe was a local merchant who built the ship workers' cottages referenced in Thompson's history. Judging from this little rhyme, my guess is that the workers were very happy to have their jobs.

Including a 1761 cobbler's cottage, which was built separately from the four ship workers' homes, these cottages are generally described as Georgian Capes, with the Coe cottages all dating from around 1800. What is a bit confounding about these homes is that they aren't identical. Most homes designed to house workers are identical, or nearly so. Let's face it; it's cheaper to do it that way. The four Coe homes, while generally similar, all have differences from one another. For example, two have upstairs dormers and two don't. Three have sidelights by the front door, while one has a transom. One house has a total of four windows flanking the front door, the others two. One very important thing they all do share (including the cobbler's cottage), according to the findings of a National Register of Historic Places report, is that "the recent additions to the rear of the houses has not changed their basic character or their contribution to the streetscape." And that is very true. Looking at them from the front is almost like looking at an undisturbed street scape from the 1800s.

Between 1779 and 1829, seventy-four oceangoing vessels were constructed at the Durham shipyard on the Oyster River. One of these shipbuilders was Joseph Coe. In addition to building ships and providing housing for his shipwrights, Coe was also a savvy entrepreneur. In 1825, he built a substantial store at the intersection of Durham's Main Street, Dover Road and Newmarket Road—the latter two making up current Route 108. The building was also near the town landing, providing a nexus for shipborne and overland transportation of goods. At a time when most stores were built of wood, Coe's was a large brick structure, making a bold statement of commercial importance and confidence. Such was the impressiveness of this building that

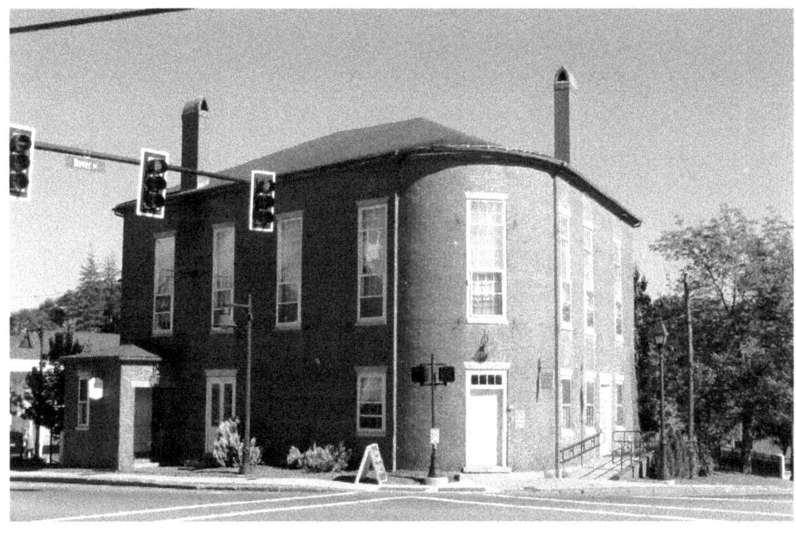

Joseph Coe's store, built in 1825. *Author's image.*

beginning in 1840, it became Durham's town hall and remained so for over a century. Today it houses the Durham Parks and Recreaction Department on the first floor and the Durham Historical Society on the second.

Joseph Coe was also very committed politically—so much that in 1840, he released a book called *The True American*. Actually, the full title is (as it appears on the title page):

The
True American;
Containing the
Inaugural Addresses,
Together with the
First Annual Addresses and Messages
of All the Presidents of the United States, from 1789 to 1839;
the Declaration of Independence, and Constitution
of the United States, with the Signers' Names;
Also, the
Farewell Addresses of Washington and Jackson;
an Address
to the Young Men of the Country,
and a
Variety of Other Matter Useful and Entertaining.

It's fair to say that pretty much covers it all.

Coe was an ardent Democrat and was anxious about the rising power of the Whigs, whom he saw as representing the interests of "wealthy aristocrats" and powerful "moneyed corporations." The tone of this book was sort of cautionary, and he hoped that it would rally young Americans to his political cause. After all, who could argue about the thoughts and words of every president? But then, just months after his book came out, disaster struck, politically speaking. Whig Party candidate William Henry Harrison (Old Tippecanoe) won the 1840 presidential election. In 1841, Coe put out another edition of his book, and with it off came the gloves. He wrote a new preface exclaiming, "The recent triumph of the Whig party has revived systems and measures which…for half a century, had been repudiated… as unsafe, unsound, inimical to liberty, and destructive of the best interest of the great mass of *people*." Elsewhere, he modestly writes of his cause: "The democratic party…approaches nearly to political perfection, because that creed identifies with universal humanity." Coe concludes his preface by stating (and speaking of himself in the third person), "Though the enemies of liberty are in power, he still confides in the intelligence and patriotism of the great body of American people, and fears not but through overruling Providence the republic will yet be preserved."

There is likely no better collection of the thoughts of all of our early leaders than *The True American*—the proof being that it is still in publication and offered on both American and European websites. And all politics aside, one can't but admire Joseph Coe's strong beliefs, love of country, entrepreneurial skills and importance in the growth of Durham. Not only was he right about the preservation of the republic, but he also saved all those people on Broth Hill from starvation!

Town Pounds

Strays, Reeves and Pounders

Impounded…one red and white heifer, with white face, red spot below the forehead, with horns, aged about 3yrs.; no brands visible.
—*newspaper impounding notice*

Just a few dozen yards north of the Joseph Coe homes on Broth Hill in Durham, the earliest recorded town pound in New Hampshire is located at the intersection of Route 108 and Durham Point Road. First built of wood in 1709, it was rebuilt in stone in 1808 and then restored in 1908. The gentleman who made the beautiful illustration of the Durham pound, Walter Nutting, in his 1923 book *New Hampshire Beautiful*, with equal grace summed up these structures:

> *The town pound of Durham, an ancient construction restored, is a good example of a custom now passed away. When every man was a farmer and every man's chief wealth was his livestock a great number of wandering cattle that broke bounds was an inevitable consequence. Some of the town-pounds are highly interesting for the height and massiveness of their walls, so that no horse, however high strung, could leap them and no bull could batter them down. It is pleasing to see here and there such an old custom recorded as in the preservation of the pound.*

Village pounds had been used in England for centuries, and for the same purposes as here in New England. (In some regions of England, they were called

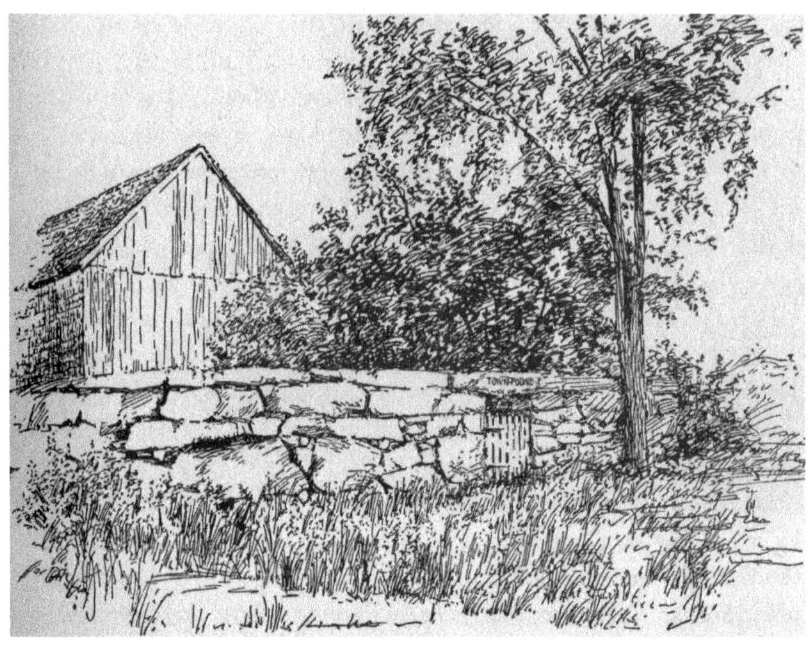

Durham Town Pound, drawn by *New Hampshire Beautiful* author Walter Nutting. *Courtesy of the Dover Public Library.*

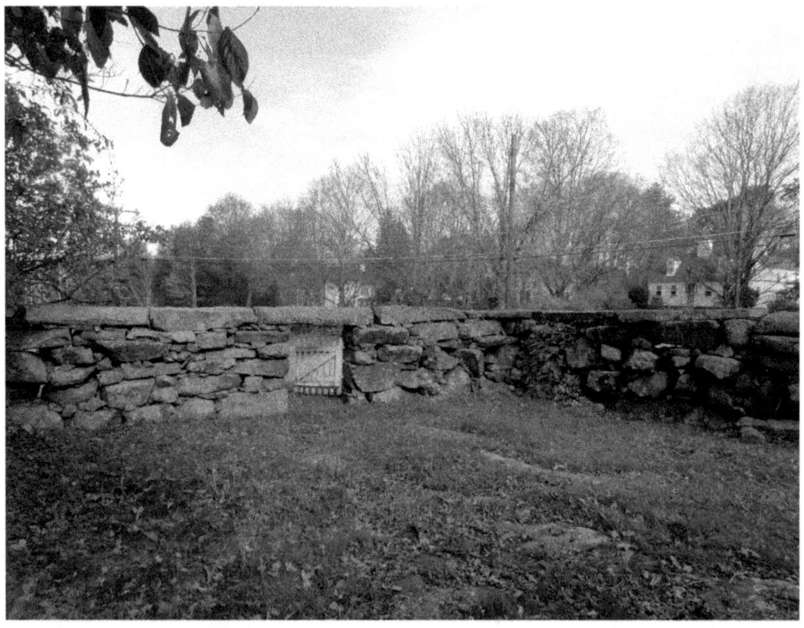

Durham pound, animal's view. *Author's photo.*

pinfolds, from the Old English *pundfald*; i.e., pound fold or pound enclosure). Generally, the common factor was that the pounds were used to hold farm animals until a fine was paid, although in England, cattle drovers would use them to hold their livestock while taking a break on the journey to market.

The construction of a town pound was one of the first civic endeavors in any new colonial town. Being that most everyone in town relied to some extent on their own livestock for survival, the need to provide grazing grounds for these animals was essential. Thus, town commons were established for this purpose with general universal rights of usage granted to townsfolk. One of our nation's oldest commons, and one that can still be visited, is, of course, Boston Common, established in 1634, just four years after the city's founding. Since by definition these common grounds were not fenced in, the potential for damage to crops or other private property by wandering animals was always present. Town pounds were therefore established to regulate animal misbehavior and to make the owners of these animals accept responsibility for any harm they caused. As new villages sprang up in outlying areas of an older town, one of the first acts of independence was to establish commons and pounds.

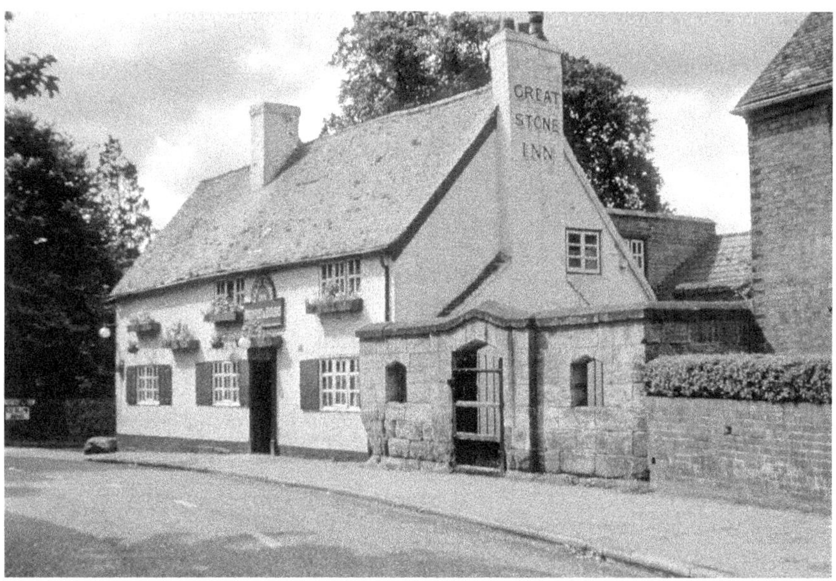

The seventeenth-century village pound in the Northfield section of Birmingham, England. It was thoughtfully built next to this much older pub—to the great delight of passing cattle drovers. Photo by Phyllis Nicklin, 1953. *Courtesy of the University of Birmingham.*

In actuality, there were two main functions of a town pound. The first had to do with nonpayment of taxes. If a landowner (virtually all of them owning livestock) failed to pay his or her property taxes, the local authorities were authorized to seize property, such as cattle, and impound it until the fines were paid. The second reason dealt with stray animals. With livestock often roaming freely or using the town common for grazing, animals causing problems or destroying property, most likely crops, would be seized and held in the pound. The offending animals would be held until restitution for any damage done was made, including any fines associated with the offense. Additionally, in both cases of impoundment, fees for the care and feeding of the animals would have to be made to the pound keeper.

A great example of how the system worked can be seen in an 1884 impounding notice from a Tasmania, Australia newspaper, the *Hobart Mercury*:

Impoundings.

PUBLIC POUND, SWANSEA.
Impounded at the above pound—
ONE RED AND WHITE HEIFER,
with white face, red spot below the
forehead, with horns, aged about
3yrs.; no brands visible.
Damages claimed, 10s.
Poundage fee, food and water, 1s 6d. per day.
If the above animal be not claimed
within the time allowed by law, it will be
sold by me on at the Public Pound,
Swansea, on 24th December at 2 o'clock.
DAVID HAYNES,
Poundkeeper.

The damages fine of 10s (shillings) would have been equivalent to U.S. $2.50 at that time. The poundage fee of 1s. 6d. (one shilling and sixpence) was equal to $0.37.5. The pound keeper, David Haynes, was originally from England. At the age of nineteen, he was convicted of stealing some linens and sentenced to seven years "transportation" (exile and confinement in a work camp) to Australia. A shoemaker by trade, Haynes was pardoned after serving six years. He stayed in Australia and rose to become the town jailer as well as pound keeper.

Impoundings.

PUBLIC POUND, SWANSEA.

Impounded at the above Pound—
ONE RED AND WHITE HEIFER, with white face, red spot below the forehead, with horns, aged about 3yrs.; no brands visible.
Damages claimed, 10s.
Poundage fee, food and water, 1s. 6d. per day.
If the above animal be not claimed within the time allowed by law, it will be sold by me on at the Public Pound, Swansea, on 24th December, at 2 o'clock.
DAVID HAYNES,
Poundkeeper.

The *Hobart Mercury* impounding notice. *Courtesy of the National Library of Australia.*

Pound keeper (sometimes known as a pounder) was generally an elected position, and it was not a bad way to make a little extra cash. A related elected position was that of hog reeve. Hogs could be especially destructive to crops, so a job was created solely for the purpose of capturing them and turning them over to the pound keeper. The reeve would also make an assessment of any damages that might need reparations. Even when the need for such a job was no longer necessary, many towns kept the hog reeve as a joke job or gave it to newly married men or to townsfolk not well liked. No matter how lofty one's former position, no one is immune from being so rewarded. John Sununu, former New Hampshire governor and chief of staff to President George H.W. Bush, was given such an honor when, upon moving to Hampton Falls in 2007, he and his wife were given the honorary titles of hog reeve and keepers of the pound.

There are dozens of town pounds still in existence and largely intact in New Hampshire, not to mention several in other New England states and as far west as California. Many pound sites around New Hampshire post a founding or construction date, but in most cases, like Durham's, the first structures were wood, to be later replaced with stone, so the structure in current existence may not date from the posted date. In New Hampshire, the Hudson and Wakefield pounds, built in 1772 and 1774, respectively, are probably the state's oldest unaltered pounds. Gloucester, Rhode Island, lays claim to the oldest original pound in New England, dating from 1749. Most pounds were rectangular, but a few were round. Milton has one of the round ones, built in 1823. In 1946, the town's residents were so concerned for its preservation when they learned that it stood in the path of a Route

16 rerouting that they had it dismantled and reconstructed out of harm's way. An especially noteworthy pound location, you will not be surprised to know, is the town of Nelson (population 729, all the way up from 721 in the first U.S. census in 1790) boasting not one, but two town pounds—proudly providing a pound to resident ratio of about 1:365.

Unfortunately, not everyone finds the preservation of these structures quite so important. In 1973, an angry landholder in Fremont (formerly known as Poplin), after winning a lawsuit about the ownership of land that the town's 1820 pound sat on, decided to celebrate his victory by taking a bulldozer to it (there is another pound in Fremont, dating from 1802, on Main Street). The good news is that, like the London Bridge Causeway in Windham, town pounds are dry stone constructions and therefore very sturdy. Even the angry Fremont property owner and his bulldozer couldn't completely destroy the Poplin pound, which is still proudly marked.

The most unusual town pound remnant is not in the seacoast area but definitely merits a mention. A stone gate standing alone on the edge of a large green field in a Manchester park is all that's left of the Derryfield pound. Technically, since by 1841, when the pound was built, the old town of Derryfield had been given its new name, it should rightly be called the Manchester town pound, but most sources refer to it as the

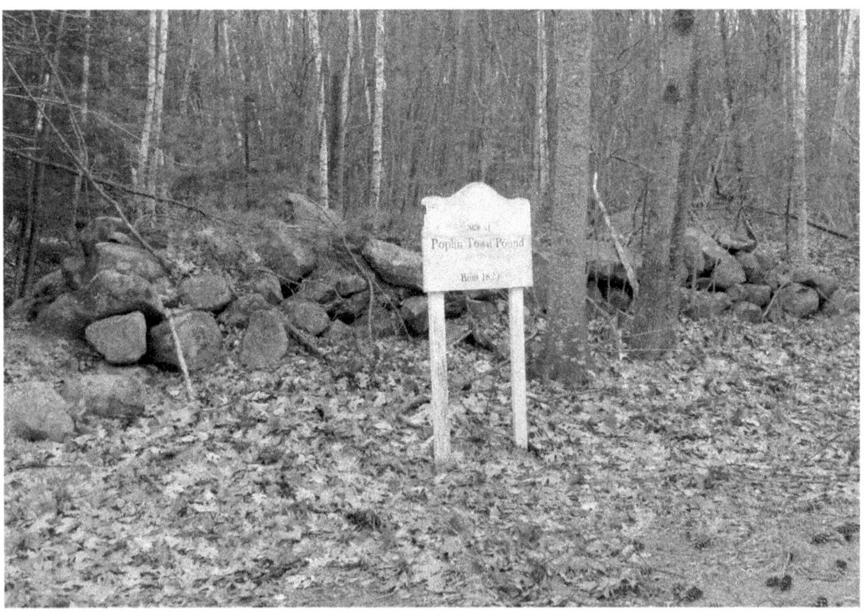

The 1820 Poplin pound, post bulldozer. *Author's photo.*

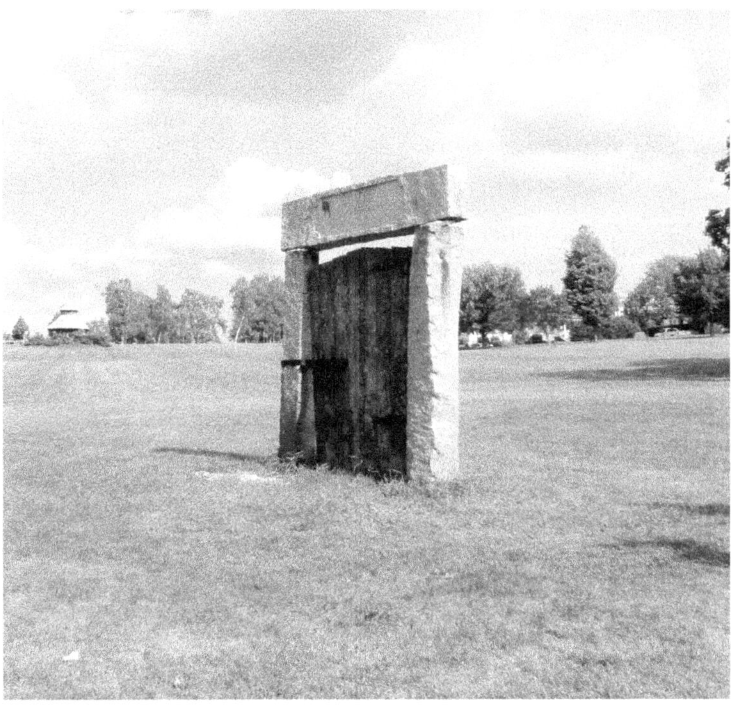

The Derryfield pound gate, which is also the marker for the final turn on the park's cross-country course. *Author's photo.*

Derryfield pound. Be that as it may, if it weren't for the local DAR, there probably wouldn't be anything left at all. The Manchester-based Molly Stark Chapter of the Daughters of the American Revolution had long been active conserving and commemorating important city sites, perhaps most importantly preserving the oldest house in Manchester, General John and Molly Stark's home on Elm Street (remember also that John Stark was the commander of…Henry Dearborn). They now use this house as their meeting place. It was in 1916 that the Molly Stark DAR placed a commemorative lintel uniting the two stone pillars of the town pound gate and therefore, in all likelihood, saving it from destruction. In the mid-'70s, the City of Manchester carted away the walls of the pound, ostensibly because of chronic vandalism to the existing stones. Were it not for that DAR lintel on top, the city probably would have carted away the gate's pillars with the rest of the stones.

The other unique thing about the Derryfield pound gate is that of all the town pounds still in existence in New Hampshire, it is the only one still performing a useful function today (although animals are no longer

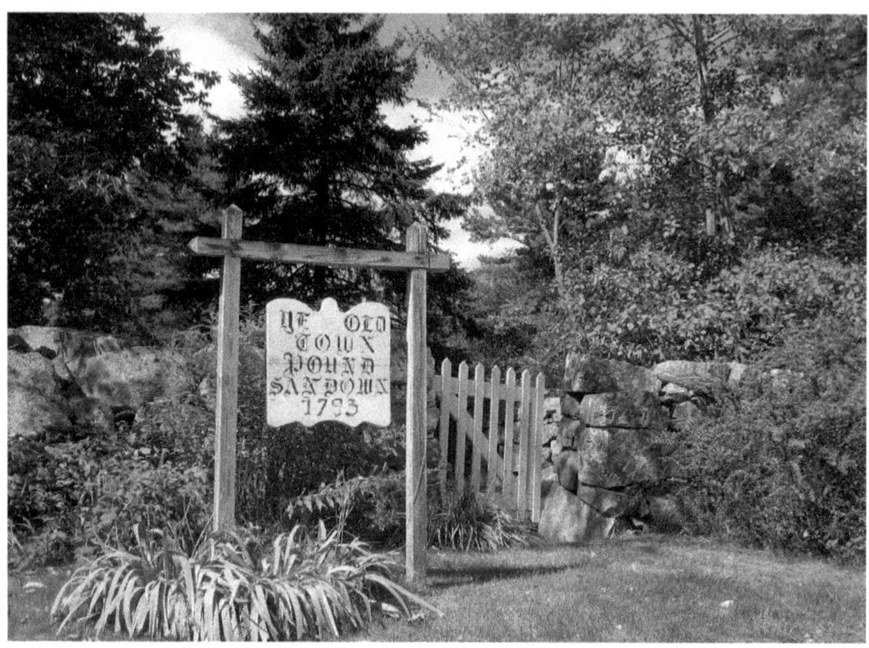

The Sandown pound on Fremont Road. Across the street is the Sandown Meeting House, one of the finest in New Hampshire, largely unaltered since its construction in 1773. *Author's photo.*

involved). Each year in the fall, hundreds of New Hampshire middle and high school students participating in cross-country meets at the Derryfield Park use the gate as a marker for the final turn in the push toward the finish line. Even better, the Derryfield Park is still used as a pound. Every winter during snow emergencies, those unfortunates who leave their cars on the streets of the Queen City may very well find them at a temporary auto pound in the park. More than likely, the fee for getting their property out is a lot more than the $2.50 charged at that Tasmanian pound.

The following is a semi-comprehensive list of remaining New Hampshire town pounds. The dates of construction of many pounds are not readily available. The dates that are given can be imprecise, as the signage at some sites shows the date of the existing pound while others use the date of the first pound built at the location—many of which have since been replaced. Additionally, sometimes the year the town voted to build the pound is given as the founding date when, in fact, the pound was built sometime later. And almost certainly there are more pounds out there.

Alstead: 1767
Atkinson: 1788
Auburn: 1853
Bedford: 1809
Bow: 1821
Bradford
Brookfield: 1806
Campton: 1816
Center Harbor: 1799
Chester: 1804
Concord:1830
Danville (originally Hawke): 1802
Derry
Dublin: late eighteenth century
Dunbarton
Durham: 1709, rebuilt 1808, restored 1908
Exeter: between 1825 and 1845
Farmington: 1802, rebuilt 1823
Fremont/Poplin (2): 1802 and 1820
Gilmanton
Hampstead: circa 1756
Hollis/Monson
Hopkinton: 1805
Hudson: 1772
Lempster: 1790
Londonderry: 1831
Loudon
Lyndborough: 1774
Madison: 1792
Manchester/Derryfield: 1841
Marlborough
Marlow
Mason: 1771
Meredith: 1789
Milton: 1823, moved 1946
Moultonborough
Nelson (2): 1783 and 1795
New Durham: 1809
New Ipswich
Pembroke
Rumney
Sanbornton
Sandown: 1793
Sutton
Tamworth
Wakefield: 1774
Wilmot: 1860
Wilton

Dover Speedway at Granite State Park

The roar of the car on the asphalt and echoing off the trees in the dark night was very exciting.... The crowd loved it.
—Nick Zipp

Granite State Park Speedway track announcer Charles A. Crocco described the culminating race of the 1958 season thus in his 1959 manuscript, *The Roaring Stock*:

> *It was a beautiful sunny bright day, October 20th, 1958, that greeted the many Stock Car Drivers who were out to capture the $500.00 New England Stock Car Racing title at "ole" Granite State Park in Dover, New Hampshire. The track looked big, just like a Roman Holiday event, and it was early afternoon as the fans began to pour in, filling the stands to a new capacity before the first race started.*
>
> *30 cars went to the post at about 3:30 pm and 30 cars on this track means that almost all of the track is filled, with little or no running room.... At the half way mark there were still 24 cars left in the race and the leader, Freddie "Butch" Schultz, had assumed a commanding lead of one lap and was beginning to lap cars.... The drivers went along quite well until the 84th lap when they were advised by the starter to run under the caution flag. This was necessary as Charlie Zipp, driving a #54 special, spun out of control on the number 2 turn of the track and his cohorts tried frantically to get him and his car back in the race without loss of laps.... Butch Schultz*

showed his exceptionally fine ability as a driver in working his way through the cars and still maintain a lead that was becoming more precious with each passing lap. With only five laps remaining Schultz seemingly was boxed into a corner but he worked his way out....Butch, driving for the Longie Stable of Lynn, was the winner in one of the finest races in years.

The closing event of the 1958 season, run before 1500 fans, will go down in local track history as one of the greatest races. Probably even better than the first track race which was held in 1864 between two women on foot. This opened Granite State Park.

Crocco's last comments might need a bit of explaining, but we'll get to that later.

Since colonial times, Willand Pond has been known variously as the Great Pond, Cocheco Pond, Humphrey's Pond, Hussey's Pond and Lake Willand. About sixty-six acres in area, it is located on the Somersworth-Dover line nestled in the corner made by Routes 108 and 9. Its first recorded use,

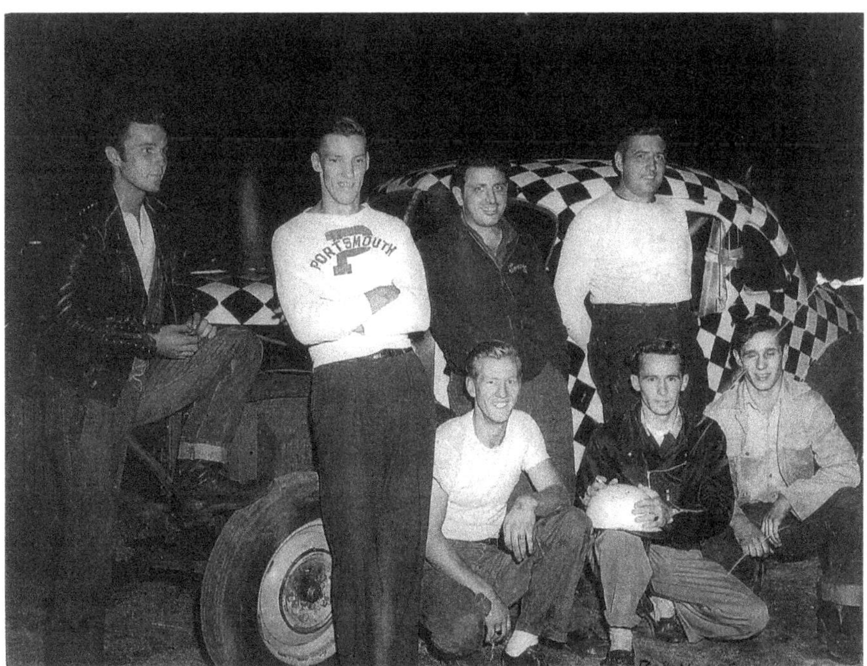

Seacoast-area drivers pose before a race in Sanford, Maine, in 1950. *Kneeling, left to right*: Ray Cormier, Portsmouth; Bob Moore, Somersworth; Dick Eon, Biddeford, Maine. *Standing, left to right*: Bob Guy, Dover; Otis Brayton, Portsmouth; Tony Colecclieo, Newington; Roger "Cowboy" Rivers, Dover, in front of his car. *Courtesy of the Summersworth Historical Society.*

from the late seventeenth century, was as a fishing camp for local Native Americans. Beginning in 1858, the New Hampshire State Agricultural Society moved its annual state fair to the northwest side of the pond at what was then called the Granite State Trotting Park in Dover (county maps show a racetrack on that site as early as 1856). In 1896, the park was bought from the Strafford County Agricultural Society by Frank Christie of Dover and Frank C. Jones, a Portsmouth millionaire known as the "King of the Ale Makers," for the purpose of building a harness racing compound.

Before getting into Granite State Park's long racing history, a bit of perspective would be useful regarding Charles Crocco's account of that 1958 championship race. The Dover track was a one-fifth-mile asphalt oval. One-fifth-mile tracks were generally designed for "Midget" racecars, but the cars in this race were much larger stock cars. For comparison, NASCAR's Daytona track is two and a half miles, the New Hampshire International Speedway's is just over one mile around and all of New Hampshire's other existing stock car circuits are at least a quarter mile. Let

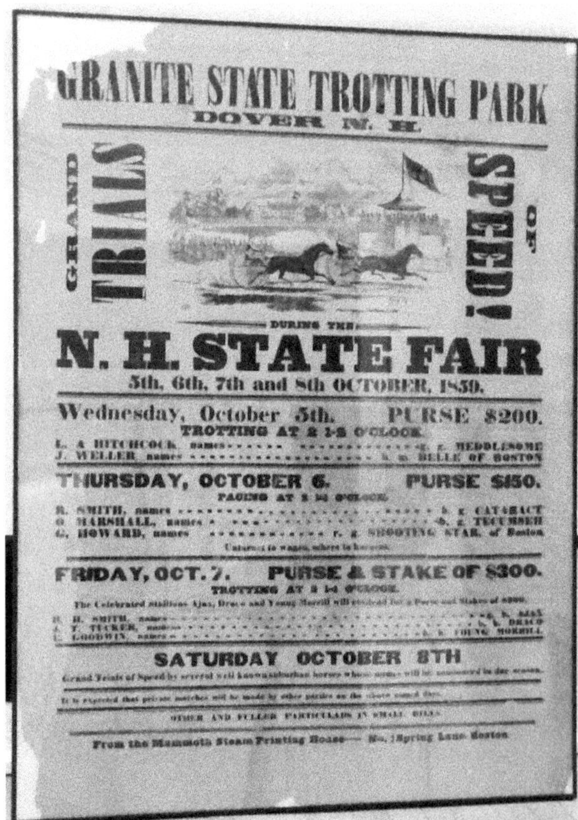

1859 New Hampshire State Fair poster at the Woodman Museum. *Author's photo with permission of the Woodman Museum collection, 182 Central Avenue, Dover.*

that sink in for a minute. Dover's oval was only about one thousand feet around and not much more than two cars wide for those thirty drivers to fight over with their pedal to the metal pretty much the whole time. So rare is a one-fifth-mile stock car track that a website dedicated to old racetracks listed Dover's, incorrectly, at a quarter mile—more than likely because no one can imagine a track so small running stock cars! (That website has now corrected the error.)

Exactly one hundred years before Charlie Crocco wrote about the big race, the first actual race was held at the Granite State Trotting Park. At the aforementioned 1858 fair, there was no formal racing, although the track was used for showing horses, cattle and the exhibition of a steam-powered fire engine. Time on the track was also provided for—believe it or not—"promiscuous driving." Disappointingly, it turns out that promiscuous driving merely meant casual, unstructured driving. In 1859, the Agricultural Society decided to jazz things up by adding four days of harness racing and speed trials on the park's one-mile oval. The state fair was held at the Granite State Trotting Park for several more years of livestock judging, harness racing and really fun joy riding before moving on to other venues.

Once Frank Jones took control of the Granite State Trotting Park, he directed his partner, Frank Christie of Dover, to begin a major upgrade. According to an 1898 history of Dover published by *Foster's Daily Democrat*:

> *In May of the same year* [1896] *Mr. Christie began making improvements....Three hundred new horse sheds have been built providing the most excellent conveniences for the stabling of horses. A steel water tower 93 feet high with a tank holding 30,000 gallons of water has been erected thus insuring a plentiful supply of pure water...throughout the Park.... Mr. Jones has also remodeled and enlarged a capacious house within the park and has furnished and equipped it as a first-class hotel and clubhouse. The Park Tavern as it has been named, has become most popular with horsemen and its success has been assured....The first race meeting was held in August, 1897. On the first day it was used, Gentry (one of two "trotters" running in a match race) went a mile over it in 2.04.*

The *Foster's* story sums things up, stating, "The track is on high land bordering a beautiful sheet of water known as 'Willand Pond.'...Granite State Park is without doubt today...the best mile track in the world over which to condition and train horses."

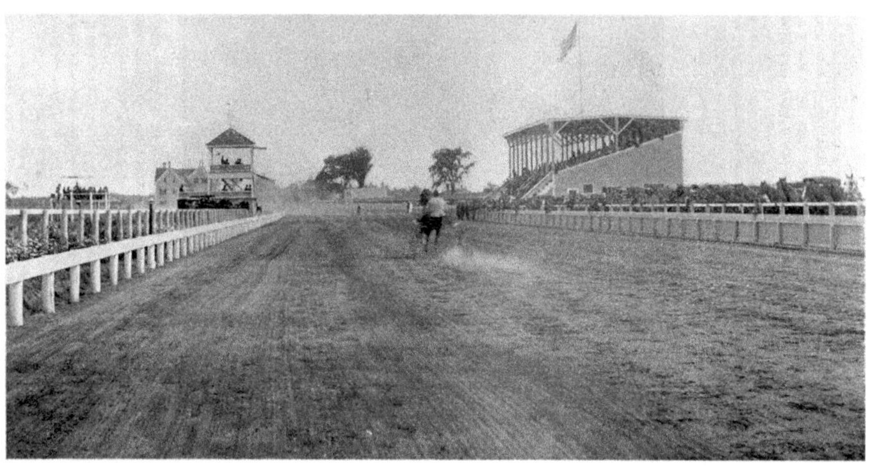

A trotter does time trails at Granite State Park in 1898. Notice that while all the humans get to sit comfortably in the grandstands, the ones having to do all the work have to watch standing on all fours by the rail on the right. Foster's Daily Democrat, *courtesy of the Dover Public Library.*

Best in the *world*! You've certainly got to love *Foster's* hometown enthusiasm. And in an example of having the perfect name for your job, the *Boston Globe*'s writer responsible for covering the ponies was none other than Frank Trott.

Barrington-born Frank Jones had a longtime interest in owning, breeding and racing horses. Although he was known as an excellent amateur reinsman, his greatest racing success and joy was in his two-thousand-acre Maplewood Farm in Portsmouth. Today, not much remains of Jones's breeding farm. His mansion still stands, located on the road named after his farm, surrounded now by homes rather than pasture, just off Woodbury Road. But in 1899, Maplewood became the top breeding stable in America, with its horses taking in over $37,000 (about $1.1 million today) in purse money and beating his nearest competing stable by $20,000.

Local histories frequently referred to Frank Jones as "the Honorable" when they weren't calling him the "King of the Ale Makers," which, of course, is honorable enough. It turns out that he earned this title when he was elected mayor of Portsmouth in 1867 and again in 1868. After that, he ran successfully for the U.S. Congress in 1874, despite being attacked by his opponent for his ale-making business, and was reelected in 1876. At any rate, he left Congress but stayed active in national politics while running his brewery. While he was at it, he also served as president of the Boston and Maine Railroad and owned the Granite State Fire Insurance Company, the Portsmouth Shoe Company, the Rockingham Hotel, the

Wentworth Hotel and, of course, Granite State Park. In 1958, he was elected to the Harness Racing Hall of Fame. Significant remnants of Jones's brewery live on today as the Frank Jones Brew Yard development off Islington Street in Portsmouth.

A little side story: In 1858, Jones began working at a brewery owned by a recently arrived Englishman named John Swindell. Swindell had immigrated to Portsmouth with an ale recipe in hopes of getting into the business. Within a few months, Jones bought out Swindell's entire share of the brewery lock, stock and ale formula. An 1881 edition of the *Granite Monthly* explained the events this way:

> *This brewery had been established a few years previously by John Swindels* [sic]...*who was a thorough master of the art of brewing, and made a superior quality of ale, but lacked the business capacity essential to success. Mr. Jones supplied that requisite and under his direction the enterprise soon gave promise of substantial returns.*

The Frank Jones Brewery went on to become one of the biggest in the Northeast. Swindell opened another brewery that turned out to be unsuccessful. On the other hand, by a single act, his life ended up making a far more significant contribution to the world.

By 1864, Swindell's second brewery attempt had failed, and he converted the plant into a shoddy factory. (At that time, the term "shoddy" meant a facility that recycled old cloth into new material.) His factory was beside a rail line that ran into Portsmouth. One evening, the engineer on the train from Concord saw a man on one side of the rails and on the other side he saw a little girl running toward the train. He reported later that he soon lost sight of both of them. After the train had passed, the little girl was found alive, but John was found dead on the tracks. The authorities determined that Swindell saved the little girl's life, and lost his, by pushing her out of the way of the train. The name of the little girl is lost from the record, but if she has any descendants, they certainly owe a debt of gratitude to John Swindell.

Under Jones, the Granite State Park became one of the premier harness racing tracks in the United States, becoming part of what was known as the Grand Circuit. Founded in 1871, the Grand Circuit is the oldest continuous horse racing series in the United States and Canada. Currently, the Grand Circuit visits twenty racecourses, including venues in New York, Ohio, Indiana, Pennsylvania, Kentucky, Delaware, Maryland and Ontario.

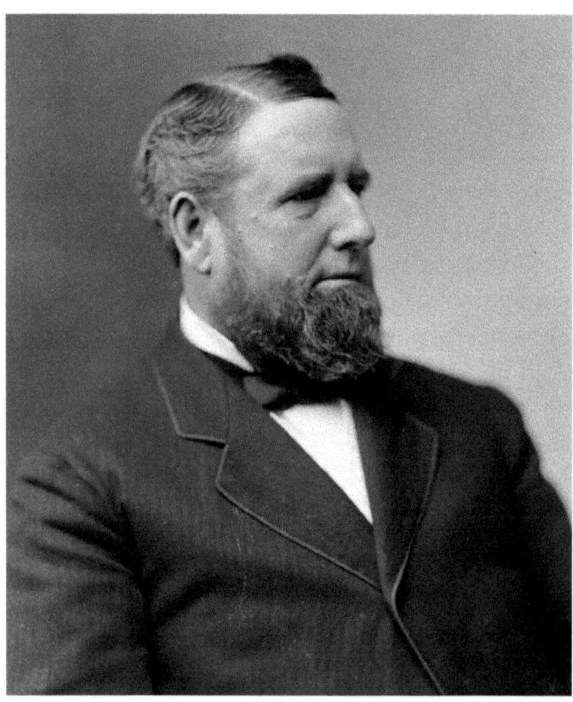

The Honorable Frank Jones, "King of the Ale Makers." *Library of Congress photo.*

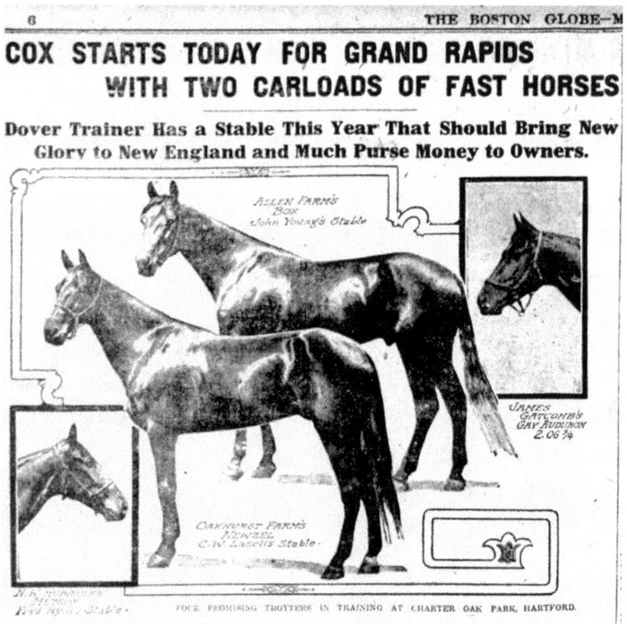

6 THE BOSTON GLOBE—M

COX STARTS TODAY FOR GRAND RAPIDS WITH TWO CARLOADS OF FAST HORSES

Dover Trainer Has a Stable This Year That Should Bring New Glory to New England and Much Purse Money to Owners.

ALLEN FARM'S
BOX
John Young's Stable

JAMES
GATCOMB'S
GAY AUDUBON
2.06 3/4

OAKHURST FARM'S
NEWZEL
C. W. Lasell's Stable

FOUR PROMISING TROTTERS IN TRAINING AT CHARTER OAK PARK, HARTFORD.

Walter Cox newspaper article from June 24, 1912. *Courtesy of the* Boston Globe.

During Granite State Park's heyday, the Grand Circuit visited Cleveland, Columbus, Detroit, Kalamazoo, Grand Rapids, Poughkeepsie, Syracuse, Hartford, Lexington and Atlanta, as well as Dover.

After Frank Jones's death in 1902, the racetrack changed hands several times. Probably the most nationally famous owner was Epsom-born Walter R. Cox, who purchased the park in 1902. Known as an outstanding reinsman and breeder, Cox's talents were sought across the nation in harness racing circles. A *Boston Globe* story from the 1912 season provides a great illustration. Walter Cox demonstrated his farsighted business acumen when he brought motorcycle racing to Granite State Park just a few years after he purchased it. Here was the ancient "Sport of Kings" sharing the stage with daredevils using the newest technology to race. The motorcycles ran on both the mile and half-mile track. Although Cox sold his interest in the park around 1920, motorcycle racing went on well into the 1950s. The December 1945 cover of *The Motorcyclist* magazine (displayed online) features three-time national

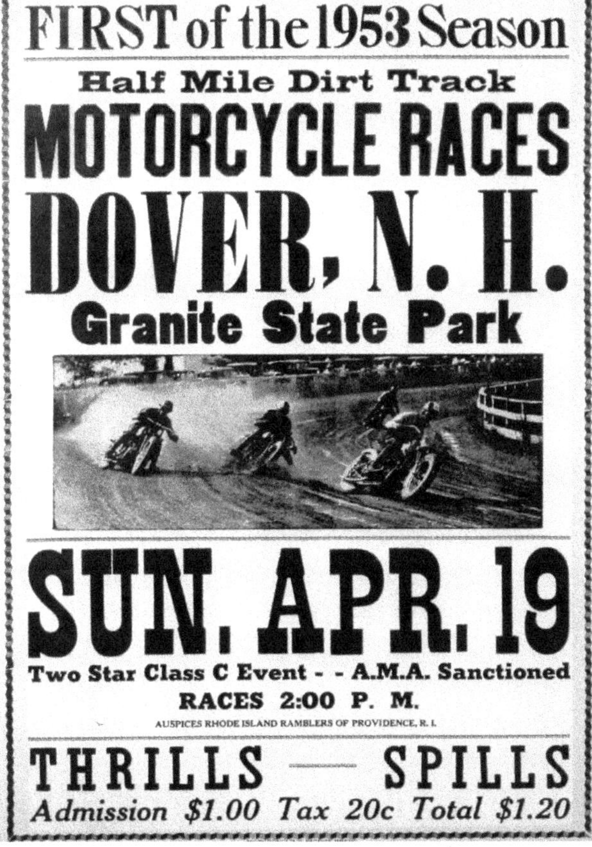

Motorcycles had been racing at GSP for over forty years by the time of this meet. *Author's collection.*

champion ('47, '48 and '49) and AMA Motorcycle Hall of Famer Jimmy Chann, as well as fellow riders Babe Tancrede and Carl Crannell in action at Granite State Park. A shipbuilder by trade, Chann went back to work at the Portsmouth Naval Shipyard in the 1950s after a career-ending injury. Rhode Island–born Babe Tancrede, also a Hall of Famer, had a day job of, naturally enough, a motorcycle patrolman in his Woonsocket hometown.

When the last harness race was run at Granite State Park in 1933, auto racing in the form of midget cars helped filled the void. Midget cars (given the slightly more sophisticated name Speedcars in Australia) are small, special-built, high power-to-weight ratio little rockets. Their wheel base is only around 70 inches, about enough length for an engine and the driver, but they have a wide track so they rarely roll. By comparison, a Ford Model A of that period had a wheel base of about 103 inches, while a modern Chevy Malibu's is about 111. Midget car racing is still a thriving sport in the United States, New Zealand, Britain and Australia. Mario Andretti, A.J. Foyt, Tony Stewart and Jeff Gordon are among the many great drivers who cut their teeth in midget racing. A story from the May 28, 1947 edition of the *Nashua Telegraph* sets the scene nicely:

> *Ace pilots from New England, New York and New Jersey will send some of the East's most costly midget auto racing plants hurtling around the Granite State Park Speedway, Dover, Memorial Day (Friday) afternoon in what is expected to be a record breaking inaugural of the 1947 NE dirt track championship campaign. All but jet-propelled, these tiny racers have taken speed fans by storm from coast to coast and the sport now rates right behind basketball, baseball and football in attendance. The Decoration Day drivers, who will be vying for points toward the NE crown, as well as the prize money, have promised an all out assault on the existing Granite State Park auto record of 68 MPH. That doesn't sound fast when you say it quickly, but when it is remembered that this speed includes skidding around four hairpin turns, it's fast traveling in anyone's book. It means that the daredevils must do close to 100 MPH on the short straightaways. The "doodlebugs" may be able to better the old mark, set by a big-car racer, because the midgets can fight their way around the unbanked curves with a minimum of braking.*

New Hampshire racing impresario Charlie Elliott became a part owner of Dover Speedway (which is mostly in Somersworth, by the way) in the early '40s. By 1948, he had gained full control of the track. As the local popularity of the midget racers waned, Charlie decided to up the excitement ante by introducing stock car racing on the recently paved one-fifth-mile oval. Suddenly, cars as big as everyday sedans—mostly Fords but also Chevys, Dodges and Hudsons—were running on a track designed for the midgets. The stock cars in those days were not quite the sophisticated machines running NASCAR circuits today. According to *The Roaring Stock*, drivers could pick up an older used car for as little as ten dollars; soup up the engine by removing the muffler and fan; and take off excess weight by stripping the inside, removing floorboards, clipping the fenders and often removing the hood. A smaller tire was usually installed on the left front to provide better cornering on a track that was mostly turns. Some of the Speedway's most exciting and colorful drivers in the late '40s and '50s included Roger "Cowboy" Rivers, Don "Juan" Prince, Bob "Beau Brummell" Moore, "Hammerin" Hank Ellsmore and Charlie and Nick Zerbinopoulos, better known as the Zipp Brothers.

Meeting Nick "Zipp," still going strong at age ninety, at his Curiosity Shop just over the border from Somersworth in Berwick, Maine, he reminisced about his racing days. He said that he got into car racing following the lead of his older brother Charlie, whom he said was much more of a daredevil. "He was the kind of kid that would ride around on his motorcycle standing up," said Nick, smiling. As previously mentioned, the Dover Speedway oval, at one-fifth of a mile, was in all likelihood the smallest stock car track in New Hampshire and even the United States, for that matter. Nick explained what it was like driving on such a small track: "It was second gear, rear-end locked the whole time. You didn't use brakes; you just let up on the gas and the locked rear wheels slowed you down" (both rear wheels are "locked" together so that they always turn in unison). He went on to say that the most exciting racing was at night: "Even though our speed usually was around sixty, under the lights with light reflecting off the car it felt like I was going a hundred miles an hour. The roar of the car on the asphalt and echoing off the trees in the dark night was very exciting....The crowd loved it."

Nick mentioned that later in their racing careers, his brother Charlie's wife did not like him to be racing so much. One night, he went on, Charlie told her that he and Nick were going to the movies when in reality they were off to race. His wife and a friend decided to take in the races themselves. When they got to their seats, they saw an overturned car on the track. Charlie's wife turned to her friend and asked, "Who's that fool on his head"? Her companion replied, "That fool is your husband!"

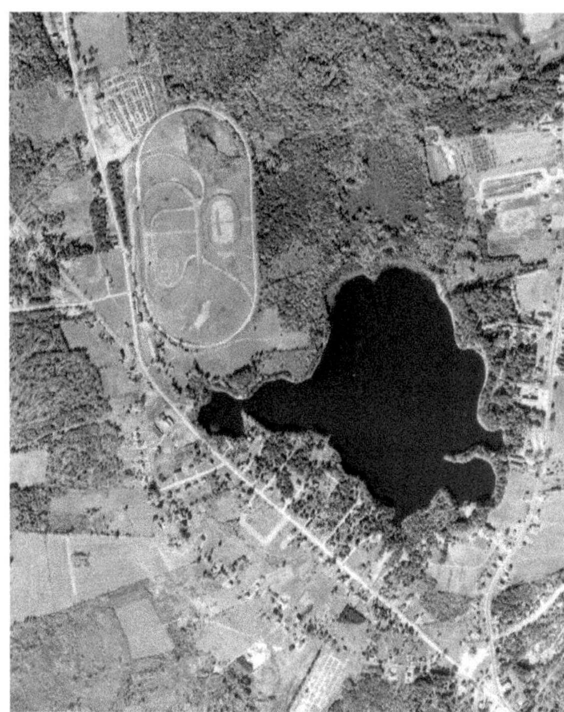

Granite State Park in 1953. Stock cars and motorcycles were still going strong. Route 108 toward Rochester skirts the left of the track, and Route 9 (High Street) skirts the right side of the pond. The old Central Park baseball field can be seen at the point where High Street runs off the image, to the left of the road. U.S. Air Force photo. *Courtesy of the Strafford County Conservation District.*

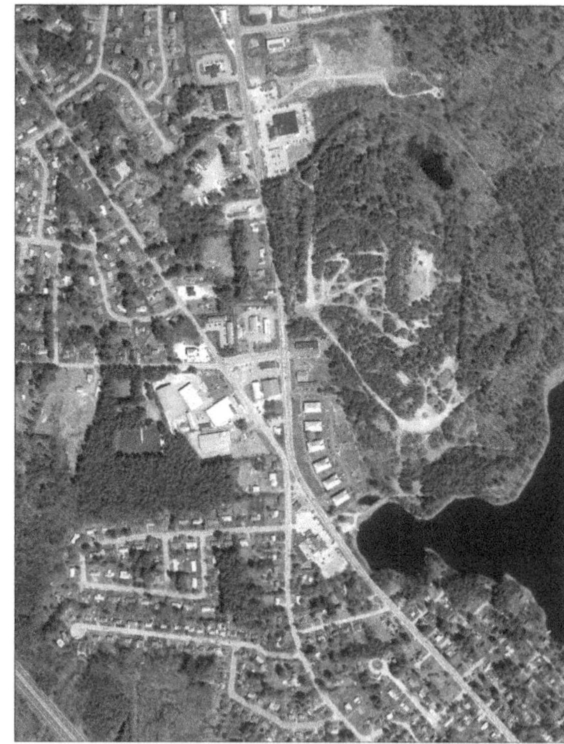

This 2015 aerial image shows the significant incursion upon the entire southwest corner of the track due to development. *Courtesy of the Strafford County Conservation District.*

The very last race of any kind at Granite State Park was held in 1965. At that time, 106 years of horse, motorcycle and auto racing came to an end. Charlie Elliott's impact on New Hampshire auto racing continued and lives on today at the Lee USA Speedway and the Star Speedway in Epping, both of which he founded and are still thrilling thousands of race fans every year. With that last race, the roar of the crowd fell silent forever. So, what's left of Granite State Trotting Park/Granite State Park/Dover Speedway? Let's do a little urban archaeology from the air.

The 1953 aerial photo clearly shows the one-mile oval, while the half mile, sharing the front straight with the mile, is visible but is somewhat obscured by other pathways. The one-fifth-mile oval is the lighter-colored area lying in the right center of the big oval. In this excellent air force photo, the pits can be clearly seen, looking like a flattened, sideways T. Looking carefully at the modern aerial photo (north is at the top), all three tracks can still be identified, albeit significantly degraded for various reasons. After the one-fifth-mile track was closed in 1965, town officials had several chunks of the asphalt track bulldozed in order to prevent unauthorized racing, allowing nature to encroach. The southwest corners of both the mile and half-mile tracks were destroyed by development projects. The good news is that there has been little degradation since this photo was taken. What's left of the half-mile track is a bit easier to see on this later image, and the lower part of the one-mile track back straight can still be clearly seen.

In a bit more urban archaeology, observe the photos showing what's left of the track today. The image of what looks like a lovely path through the woods is actually the back straight of the original mile, dating from at least 1856. In the image of the wooden posts, you can see a small portion of the front straight retaining wall, the entirety of which is clearly visible to the left of the cars in the action photo. That any of the asphalt on the one-fifth mile is still intact is rather amazing when one considers how fragile asphalt can be when left out in the elements untended for fifty years. Ironically, those same bulldozers that cut up the track more than likely helped to keep the rest of it from being torn up by illicit racing. That '53 aerial photo was during the zenith of stock car racing at Dover Speedway when Charlie and Nick Zipp, Cowboy Rivers and their friends were tearing it up.

And what of Charlie Crocco's story of the first-ever race at Granite State Park—the one "between two women on foot" in 1864? Unfortunately, Charlie's not around to tell us how he came by that information. However, earlier in his *The Roaring Stock* Charlie referenced that same race as being "between two females who brought racing to Granite State Park" as

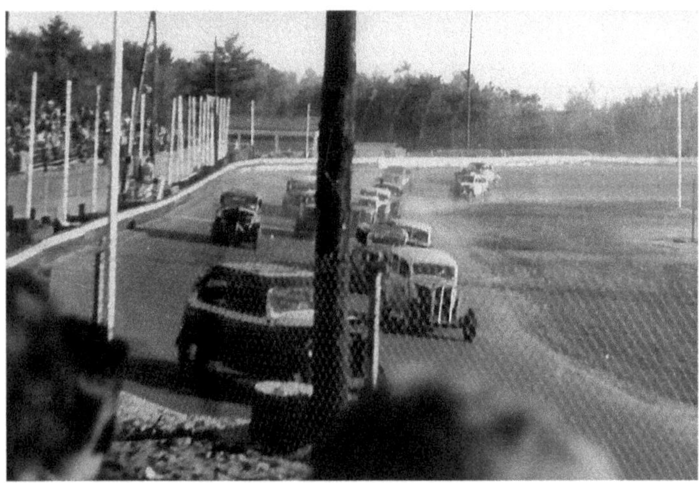

Heading into turn one at Dover Speedway, early 1950s. *Courtesy of Steve Desharnais.*

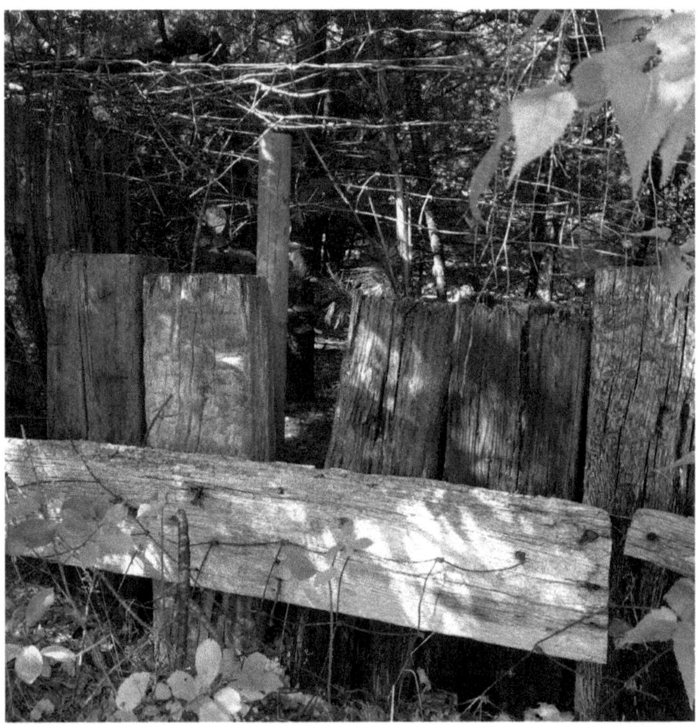

Remains of the Dover Speedway retaining wall on the front straight. *Author's photo.*

opposed to the "two women on foot" he mentioned later. After much digging around, it was discovered that many early harness races held at GSP were match races—that is, between just two horses. In many of these races, the horses were listed in the program by their names and then their gender. Therefore, "two females" often would indeed race against each other. Cutting Charlie a bit of slack on the date, off by only a few years, one can see how a story like his could take root. And since Charlie's not here to defend himself, who's to say that such a race as he described didn't happen? Either way, his colorful description of those thirty stock cars scorching the asphalt on that sunny day in 1958 certainly proves that it was indeed one of the greatest races ever held!

The term "rescue" in archaeological parlance generally is not, as one might expect, an effort to save a historical site in danger of destruction but rather the effort to "rescue" and record vital information about a site facing imminent destruction before that information is lost. This story isn't about anything close to that sort of archaeological intervention, but it is unique as compared to the other nine stories in this book. All the sites referenced in this book, except the racetracks in this story, are safe from harm and can be either visited or openly observed. The remains of Granite State Park/

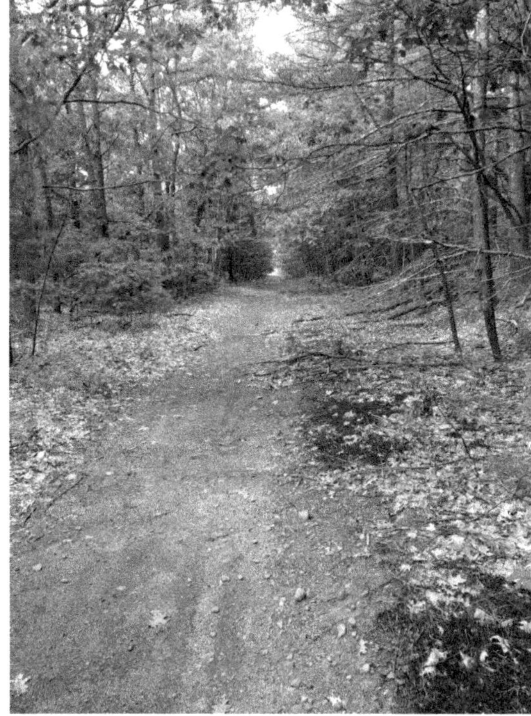

The back stretch of the original one-mile racetrack—where hooves once thundered, now a quiet walk in the woods. Maps show a track there by 1856. *Author's photo.*

Dover Speedway, on the other hand, are somewhat hidden away on private land that is for sale. Even a track as nationally famous as Rockingham Park in Salem (which gets a shout-out in the Oscar-winning movie *The Sting*) is not immune to development, as it has now been demolished for retail and residential use. The good news is that the land on which GSP sits has been up for sale for several years and so may be around for a while more. But eventually it will be sold and developed. All that flat, open land is just too tempting a target. Hopefully, however, this chapter will help a little bit to keep alive the stories of Walter Cox, Jimmy Chann, Nick Zipp and all the others who raced here—including those "two women" in 1864.

Author's note: Not long after his interview, the sad news arrived that Nick "Zipp" Zerbinopoulos had suddenly taken ill and passed away. Dover-born Nick was so much more than a stock car driver and great storyteller. In addition to his racing, he was also a champion candlepin bowler, a skill in which he took great pride. He was a World War II army veteran, and after his racing career, he became a top salesman, initially for a bread company and then for automobiles. Eventually, he owned his own businesses, first Nick Zipp Auto Sales in Newington and then, for over forty years, Nick's Curiosity Shop in Berwick. The world was a better place for having Nick in it, and he will be missed.

Atkinson Academy

America's Oldest

Above all things I hope that the education of the common people will be attended to.
—Thomas Jefferson, letter to James Madison, 1787

There probably aren't too many classrooms still in use that had kids sitting in them when Thomas Jefferson was president. The Timberlane Regional School District was formed in 1966 when the towns of Atkinson, Danville, Plaistow and Sandown combined to send their elementary students to a common high school. All of Timberlane's elementaries are pleasant, welcoming buildings, but the drive up the quiet lane to Atkinson Academy is a different experience altogether. Instead of the usual postwar baby boom, single-story brick elementary school typically seen from Maine to California, Atkinson Academy is the quintessential New England stately public edifice. And if that isn't enough, the simple sign hanging out front is a traffic stopper—at least for those paying attention. Built in 1803…second co-educational school in America…this is pretty big stuff tucked into a quiet corner of the Granite State. Who would have thought that there were *any* non-collegiate school buildings that old still being used for everyday classroom instruction? And as it turns out, there aren't many. Maybe none, other than AA (as it was frequently called). More importantly, being the second co-ed school in the country is certainly very impressive. The first co-educational school in the United States was the Leicester Academy in Massachusetts, founded in 1783. In 1867, it merged with Leicester's public high school, so Leicester

Academy's legacy of co-ed education lives on today as Leicester High—but its early building is long gone.

Academies started to spring up around New England after the Revolution as a college prep complement to the common schools, which had been in existence since early colonial days. The common schools were early public schools set up by towns to provide the basic three Rs for the largely rural children of colonists. Academies, on the other hand, were private institutions designed to prepare students for admission to colleges. Academy students were not only locals, but they could be from neighboring towns, states or even other countries. Literature, advanced mathematics, science, Latin and Greek, as well as piety and virtue, among many other subjects, were offered, and students usually had to pay tuition to attend. Unlike many academies, which were often founded or underwritten by a generous benefactor, Atkinson Academy was a town effort led by three men: the Reverend Stephen Peabody, Dr. Nathaniel Peabody (a distant relative of Stephen) and Dr. William Cogswell. Since there was no wealthy benefactor, the academy was supported by donations of land for the building, monetary donations from townsfolk, volunteer construction labor, lotteries, state land grants and tuition—which initially was one dollar per quarter.

A visit to Atkinson Historical Society's Kimball House Museum, just a few yards down the road from the academy, is a fascinating experience. Adele Dillon, a member of the society and one of the museum's curators, has a wealth of knowledge about the academy as well as Atkinson town.

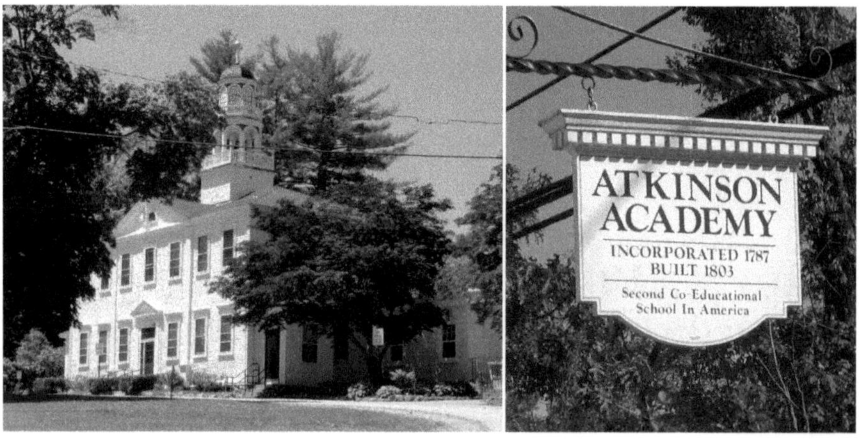

Left: Atkinson Academy. *Author's photo.*

Right: Author's photo.

According to Adele, the three academy founders had all served as officers in the Revolutionary War and had been struck by the lack of literacy among many of the rank and file troops. Therefore, all three men felt strongly that now that a democracy was in place, the need for an educated electorate was crucial in order for the democracy to survive.

Atkinson was a town with strong revolutionary fervor. At the outbreak of war, each man in town signed this pledge: "We do hereby solemnly engage and promise that we will, to the utmost of our power, at the risk of our lives and fortunes, with arms oppose the hostile proceedings of the British fleets and armies against the United American Colonies."

The academy's three founders were all actively engaged in the war effort. The Reverend Stephen Peabody, when he wasn't preaching, was a farmer who raised horses and cattle, built his own stone walls and was known to ride through the parish singing from horseback. He had been living in Atkinson only a few years when he was called to duty as an army chaplain. Dr. Nathaniel Peabody was also a military man. In 1774, he was awarded a Crown commission as lieutenant colonel of the Seventh New Hampshire Regiment, but soon after he became the first British officer in the state to resign his commission because of his political principles—he could no longer serve the Crown. He eventually rose to the rank of major general of the New Hampshire militia, replacing John Cilley in that position in 1793. While he was at it, he was one of the principal founders of the New Hampshire State Medical Society. Dr. William Cogswell left home at

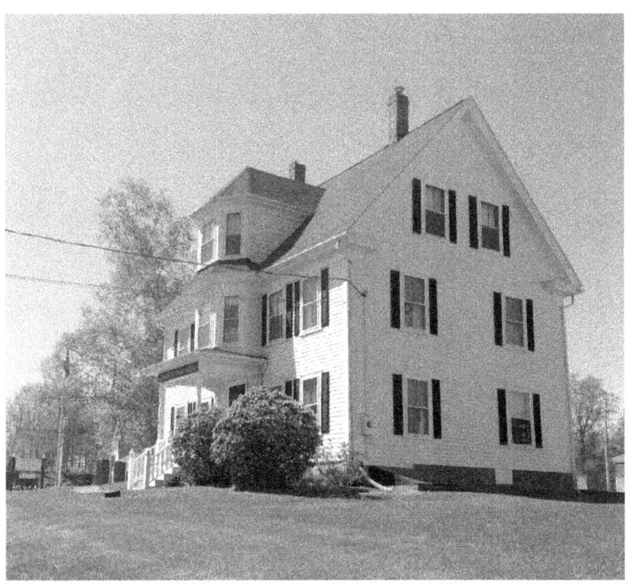

Reverend Stephen Peabody's home (1772), now the home of the Atkinson Historical Society. Two of President John Adams's grandchildren boarded here while attending the academy. *Author's photo.*

age twelve to study medicine with his brother-in-law, but in 1776, at the age of fifteen, he enlisted in the army of the United States in a company commanded by his brother, Thomas. After a year, he returned to his studies. In 1781, he was made surgeon's mate at the General Military Hospital at West Point, and by 1784, at the age of twenty-four, he became the chief medical officer of the United States regular army.

In 1787, the same year as Jefferson's plea to James Madison quoted on the title page, the efforts of these three gentlemen paid off with the opening of the Atkinson Academy (Jefferson and Madison had been corresponding with each other discussing ideas for the new republic as the Constitution was being written). Four years later in June 1791, Polly, the daughter of the Reverend Stephen Peabody, along with Hannah Atwood, Elizabeth Knight and Lucy Poor, enrolled at the academy. The second co-ed school in the United States was born. According to an 1894 article in *The New England Historical and Genealogical Register*:

> *The tradition is that "Polly" Peabody told her father that she was going to the academy. He was amazed at such a proposition, for up until that time but few girls had received more than an elementary education, but he could deny his only daughter nothing, and she and some of her companions were admitted, sat with the boys, joined their classes, and co-education was established. The advocates of women's rights should give merited credit to "Polly" Peabody and Atkinson Academy for this advance movement in the higher education of women.*

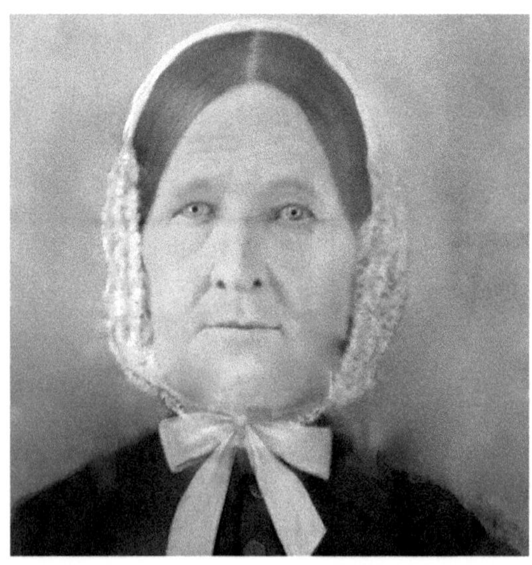

Polly Peabody, painted as an adult, in a portrait commissioned by one of her sons. It hung for many years at the academy. *Courtesy of Steven Lewis of the Atkinson Historical Society.*

In August of that year, Miriam Emerson, Polly Gordon and Sally Webster joined them, followed by Mehitable Carlton, Polly Dummer, Deborah Moody and Mehitable Moody in September. The building in which these young women joined their male classmates was begun in 1786. The land for the building was donated by Dr. Cogswell. Reverend Peabody did his part as he reported in his diary that on September 21 of that year, when work was nearing completion, "I went over and gave them a bottle of rum in grog. On the 23d the frame is up and they are boarding it fast." "Rum in grog" simply means rum (or any spirit) in water. Apparently, if one is going to give it to construction workers on a job site, a very precise formula is necessary in order to avoid crossing the line from working fast to falling asleep. At any rate, the one-story building, with a reported large chimney and spacious fireplace, was ready for the academy's opening in 1787.

In the early days, the course of studies available to the girls included reading, grammar, geography, composition and public speaking. Additionally, girls had the option of taking embroidery and painting classes. But by 1837, it appears that classes were offered equally between girls and boys without restriction, as an enrollment list from that year shows students of both sexes taking such classes as Greek and Latin. The education of females did not often sit well. No less a luminary than John Adams wrote to his daughter Abby, who was studying Latin (in Massachusetts), around 1780: "This will do you no harm, my dear, though you must not tell many people of it, for it is scarcely reputable for young ladies to understand Latin and Greek." And this letter appeared in the *Haverhill Guardian of Freedom* newspaper shortly after the Atkinson Academy held its annual exhibition (a public performance where students would showcase their knowledge, original writing and speaking skills) on October 22, 1793:

> *The ostentatious account of the exhibition at Atkinson, published in your last Friday's paper, excites in a correspondent the desire to know for what purpose the female pupils of the Academy in that town are taught ORATORY, or the art of public speaking? The utility of instructing male students to speak in public is generally acknowledged. But as women are not permitted to speak, either in the pulpit, or at the bar* [presenting in court], *what propriety is there in teaching them that branch of education? Do the trustees of the seminary expect...to be able to furnish the superb THEATRE now erecting at Boston with actors of both sexes?*

The emphasized words were the letter writer's doing. It's probably fair to say that this overwrought correspondent was not being complimentary to either the theater or actors—but he did produce a pretty good example of an early tweet.

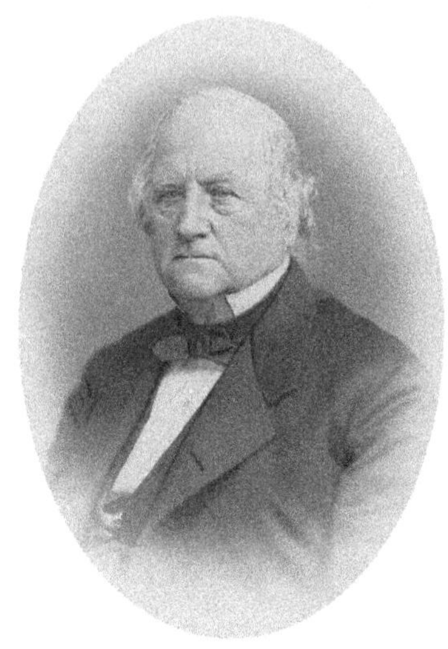

Atkinson alum Governor Edward Kent of Maine. *Courtesy of the Maine State Archives.*

There were those, of course, who were pleased with the co-ed nature of the academy. Looking back, Atkinson alum and two-time Maine governor Edward Kent (1838–39, 1841–42) wrote, "If I were to be a boy again and go to Atkinson Academy, I should hope to meet the young, intelligent and pure girls whose presence and society did so much to mend the manners and improve the hearts of the somewhat rough specimens of incipient manhood on the opposite benches."

There is very little record of the overall reaction to the inclusion of girls into the academy and virtually nothing from the students of the time. In her 1940 history, *Atkinson Academy*, Mary Webster Marr, a one-time academy teacher, writes, "The admission of girls into the Academy took place without any great excitement." Somehow, that seems quite appropriate. School kids, then and now, tend to take for granted what is presented to them, even something seen as unusual and historic when looking back. To the credit of students throughout the ages, most things are simply accepted at face value.

By the mid-nineteenth century, Atkinson Academy was thriving. In 1802, the first academy building was destroyed by fire, but within a year, the beautiful new (and current) building was completed. In 1837, the course offerings had expanded to Greek and Latin grammar, rhetoric, English grammar, logic, geography, arithmetic, algebra, Euclidian geometry, navigation, philosophy, chemistry and astronomy—the latter subject written by AA alum and longtime preceptor John Vose. The tuition was now three dollars per quarter. In 1850, the 2,000th student had passed through its portals.

A preceptor is basically a teaching headmaster, and John Vose was one of Atkinson's most revered. John was born in 1766 in very rural Bedford. As a student, he boarded at Reverend Peabody's house (two of President John

Adams's grandsons boarded at Peabody's house as well while they attended the academy). When some of the city boys staying there poked fun at his country manners and clothing, Reverend Peabody admonished them, saying, "If I mistake not, that boy will outstrip you all." Vose graduated Phi Beta Kappa from Dartmouth and then, in 1795, returned to Atkinson Academy to serve as preceptor for the next twenty-five years. He then spent eleven years as preceptor at Pembroke Academy before returning to live out his days in Atkinson, serving on the AA's board of directors. In the meantime, he wrote two astronomy textbooks and served a term as state senator and then another as a state representative. Two of his daughters, Elizabeth and Martha, also led the academy as preceptresses.

These days, Adele Dillon, or any other of the society's enthusiastic volunteers, will proudly give a tour of the Kimball House Museum (it's

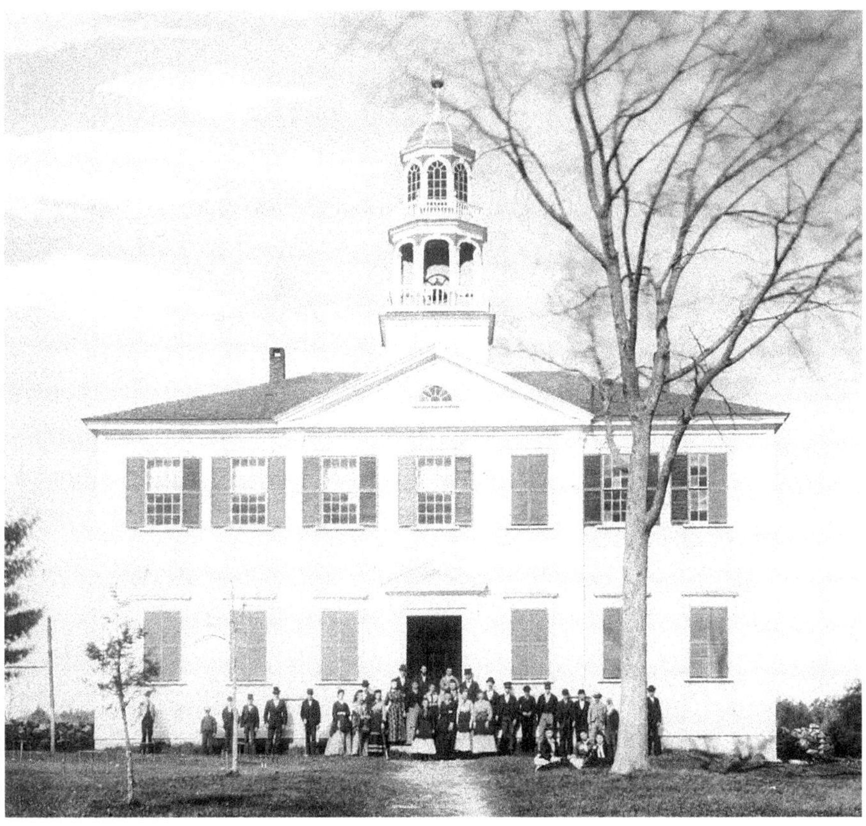

Academy students and faculty posing in an undated photo but thought to be in the late nineteeth century, according to local sources. *Courtesy of the Atkinson Historical Society.*

open one day a week and one extra Saturday per month). It is loaded with academy artifacts and mementos as well as town treasures. The building in which it is housed was not only Reverend Stephen Peabody's home but later on became the town's library until a beautiful new one was built next door in 2008. There are many remnants of the building's life as a library still intact, but the best of them is a delightful, colorful mural on the walls and ceiling in what was the children's corner. The museum contains many fascinating artifacts of the old days—an enrollment list for the 1818 school year, an 1858 grammar textbook, to name a couple—but the most intriguing has to be a phrenology bust. As a schoolboy in the 1790s, Austrian physician Franz Joesph Gall noticed that fellow classmates with really good memories seemed to have large foreheads and prominent eyes. That observation led him to theorize that an organ of memory function must lie behind the eyes. He then assumed that other abilities must be indicated by external features as well. Congenital bumps or depressions on the head and even the shape of the head were thought to be predictors of intellectual and emotional traits. Phrenology became well accepted worldwide, and especially in America.

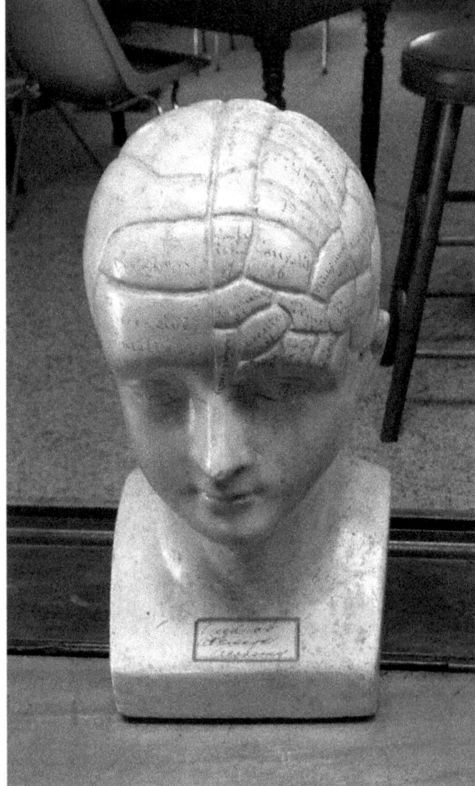

A phrenology bust once used at AA, now in the Historical Society's Kimball House Museum. *Author's photo with permission of the museum.*

By the late nineteenth century, however, it had been largely discredited, although some ideas have stuck. Terms such as "highbrow," "lowbrow" and "well rounded" all came to us from phrenology. And Dr. Gall was one of the first scientists to understand that emotions are a brain function as opposed to originating in other organs, such as the heart, as was commonly believed.

Speaking of science, judging by this abstract of a 1925 article published in the British scientific journal *Nature*, at least one Atkinson grad was involved in real science:

> *ONE of us (R.A.S.) in a study of pp 'groups in atomic spectra, which will be published in full later, has observed that in many two-valence-system spectra the frequency of the first pp 'group is nearly a mean between the frequency of the first line of the principal series of singlets in the spectrum and the first line of the principal series of doublets of the once more ionized atom.*

Well, that's easy for that abstract's writer to say. The "R.A.S." mentioned in the *Nature* abstract is Ralph A. Sawyer: Atkinson Academy, 1911; Dartmouth, 1915; University of Chicago, 1919 (PhD in physics). His doctorate from Chicago came after he had dropped out for a year during World War I to join the navy, where he designed optical instruments for the Bureau of Ordnance. Upon leaving the University of Chicago, he was hired as a physics instructor at the University of Michigan. He ended up staying there for the next forty-five years and attained the position of dean of Michigan's Horace Rackham Graduate School, among dozens of other posts and honors. He again served his country in the naval reserve during World War II, entering in 1941 as a lieutenant commander, and then again after the war when, in 1946, he became the civilian technical director of Operation Crossroads. This operation, where Dr. Sawyer supervised five hundred scientists, was tasked with the testing of atomic bombs at Bikini Atoll. From 1951 to 1959, he was made director of the Michigan Memorial Phoenix Project, a university effort to promote the peaceful use of nuclear energy—a program that is still going strong at U of M. Despite his leadership in such fields as spectroscopy, hyperfine structure of spectral lines and quantitative spectrographic analysis, as well as traveling the world on scientific endeavors and his commitment to education in Ann Arbor, Ralph Sawyer never forgot his connections eight hundred miles to the east at the academy. In 1937, on the 150th anniversary of Atkinson Academy's founding, Dr. Sawyer was named first president of the newly formed Alumni Association. As it turned out, the timing of the founding of this new alumni group was none too soon.

By the early twentieth century, local public high schools began to have class offerings that in earlier times would have been limited to the academies, including Atkinson. As a result, the school's enrollment began to decline. Around 1925, the academy underwent remodeling to accommodate overflow students from Atkinson's Center School, which rented a classroom there. Finally, in 1949 the academy closed its doors. The trustees donated the building to the town, but it stood idle for several years and began to deteriorate—to the point that razing it began to be discussed. It was at this time that the Alumni Association stepped in, raising $3,000 to shingle the roof, repair the tower and plaster classrooms. In 1955, when the renovations were completed, Louise Burnham, a past president of the Alumni Association, penned a poem to commemorate the occasion. The first stanza goes like this:

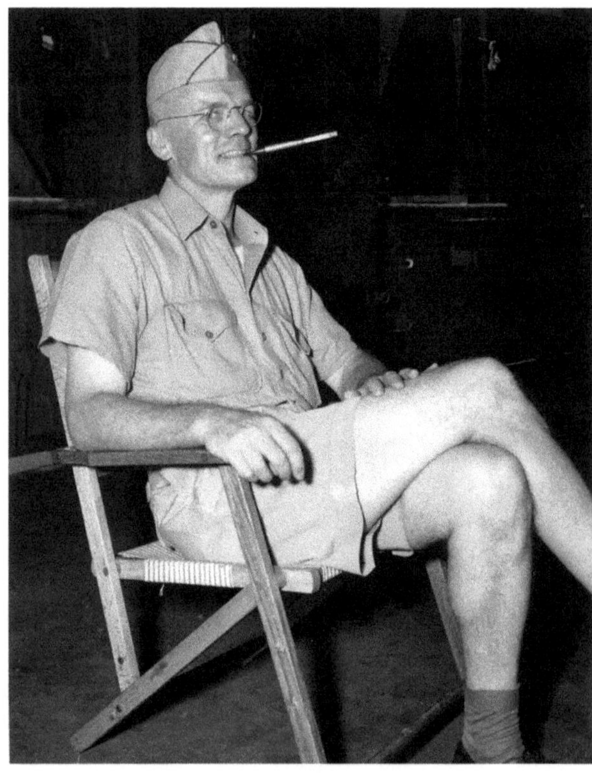

Academy alum Dr. Ralph Sawyer apparently channeling his inner FDR while on duty at Bikini Atoll in 1946. *Courtesy of the Bentley Historical Library, Ralph A. Sawyer Collection, University of Michigan.*

What, tear this dear old building down
That was second in the nation
To open wide its sacred doors
For female's education?

The building was saved, and in 1956, with Atkinson's school population booming, it again was receiving students—this time as a public elementary school for the town's children, along with the recently opened Rockwell School. The academy has been thriving ever since. Over the years, other buildings have been added to form a modern learning campus. From 1979 through 1981, UNH professor Dr. Donald Graves conducted a groundbreaking study of children's writing at the academy. The study drew hundreds of educators from across the country to learn about the school's writing process. The outcome of this study was his book *Writing: Teachers & Students at Work*. As a result, since then students' writing assignments across the nation and beyond have generally been about getting their thoughts down on paper, rather than worrying about outlines or grammar first. In 1988, Atkinson Academy became the town's sole school.

Without doubt, the 1803 building at the academy is the oldest school building in America where girls and boys have continually taken instruction together, as is proudly stated on the school's website. The first U.S. college to go co-ed was Oberlin College in Ohio in 1833, so the AA has that beat by decades. Atkinson Academy could also very well be the oldest K–12 building of *any* type still used as an everyday classroom. There are many schools as institutions older than AA, with Boston Latin, established in 1635, as America's oldest. But in most cases, those schools' early buildings have long since been demolished or, if they do still stand, have ceased to be used for everyday instruction. Wren Hall, at the College of William and Mary, in Williamsburg, Virginia (reportedly designed by Sir Christopher Wren, architect of St. Paul's Cathedral in London), has been used as a classroom since 1716, but this, of course, is a college. It turns out there are quite a few very old former K–12 classroom buildings still being used for academic purposes. For example, in South Berwick, Maine, Berwick Academy's first classroom building, the 1791 House, was used for daily instruction until the 1820s and is still serving the school as an administrative building. But it has been without classrooms for nearly two hundred years. Extensive searching turned up no evidence of any other K–12 building in the United States that has been continuously used for daily instruction longer than

AA's 1803 building. That schoolhouse might be out there somewhere, but given the fact that most schools outgrow and abandon older buildings, it seems unlikely.

Today's students attending class in Atkinson Academy's original building more than likely don't sit around and think about the history all around them—which is as it should be. Atkinson Academy's 1803 building is not a museum or artifact; it is a living learning center with teachers still providing lessons and children still learning. Thomas Jefferson would be very proud.

New Hampshire's Central Park

The trip around the lake is a most delightful one.
—Union Street Railroad advertisement

A few years before harness racing went big time on the northwest side of Willand Pond, another big entertainment complex was taking root across the water. Henry W. Burgett, owner of the Union Street Railway, with tracks running by the east side of what was then called Hussey's Pond, laid out plans for an elaborate amusement park on the pond's shore. Beginning in the mid-nineteenth century, "trolley parks" sprang up along street railway routes all over the country. Trolley companies would build them to drum up ridership on weekends. At their peak in the early years of the twentieth century, there were over one thousand trolley parks dotting the American landscape. Famous amusement parks such as Steeplechase Park on Coney Island and Palisades Park in New Jersey were trolley parks. Today there are only around a dozen such parks left—New Hampshire's Canobie Lake, established in 1902, being one of them. New Hampshire at one time had four trolley parks. In addition to Canobie Lake, there was the Contoocook River Amusement Park near Concord, the Pine Island Park in Manchester and Central Park, mostly in Somersworth but with a sliver in Dover.

Burgett purchased the Dover Horse Railway (DHR), as well as twenty-seven acres on the pond next to the railway line that ran from Dover to Somersworth, in August 1889 from Dover resident and railroad president

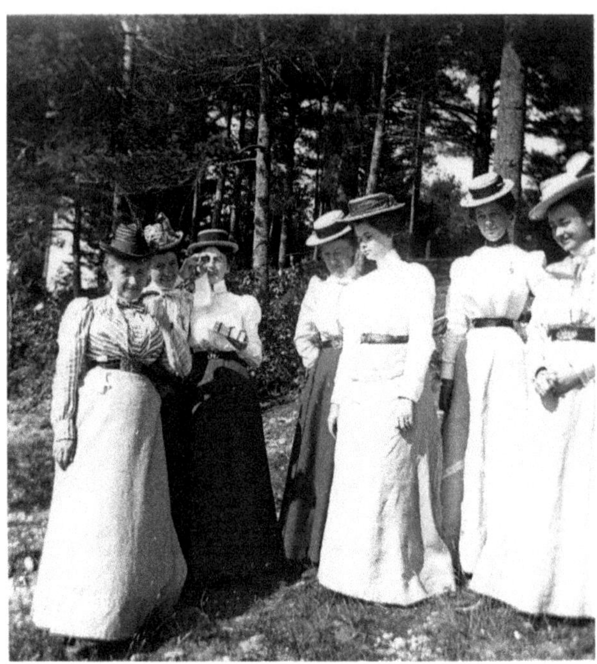

Enjoying Central Park on a summer's day, circa 1900. *Courtesy of the Summersworth Historical Society.*

Mary Dow. The fact that Mrs. Dow was the president of a railroad had made her quite a celebrity. She had been a minority stockholder in the company (and was wise enough to buy property along the DHR's right of way) when she learned that a Boston syndicate was attempting to buy up shares in order to take control of the railroad. Rather than allow the railroad's profits to leave town, she outmaneuvered the syndicate and ended up with 51 percent of the shares. In January 1888, the board of directors elected her president, thereby making her the first woman president of a railroad in the world. Considering that this event put her in a class with such hard-charging railroad tycoons as Cornelius Vanderbilt, Jay Gould and Leland Stanford, you can see why this was a very big deal in 1880s America. The fact that the Dover Horse Railroad was not quite in the same league as the New York Central didn't seem to matter too much. Dozens of newspapers from around the country and around the world heralded this event, including the *New York World*, *London Illustrated Press* and, believe it or not, the *Phrenological Journal*. That august publication featured her, along with railway car magnate George Pullman, in its December 1889 issue as part of a special feature called "Notable People of the Day." The article examined both of them from a phrenological point of view, i.e. head bumps and facial features. Fortunately, their stories in such a dicey publication didn't seem to harm either one's career, as Pullman became one of America's wealthiest men and Mary Dow was presented to the United States Congress and invited to the White House to meet with President Grover Cleveland.

One of Mary Dow's first moves as president was to raise employees' pay and lower fares from six cents to five cents. Within a year, she had moved the railroad from a position of being in debt to having its stock pay a 20 percent dividend. Share values increased nearly twenty-fold. She introduced a ticket system for rides and had a tobacco company pay for the printing of them in exchange for advertising on the back side. Since Dow had spent some time living on a farm, she knew horses and therefore bought *and* took care of them for the railroad.

Our story of Mary Dow could rightfully end here except for the fact that she was pretty much a combination of Susan B. Anthony, Ben Franklin and the "Most Interesting Man in the World" from commercial fame. Born in 1848, in her twenties she moved to St. Louis to teach French and German in a girls' academy. While there, she performed as a successful actress, sharing

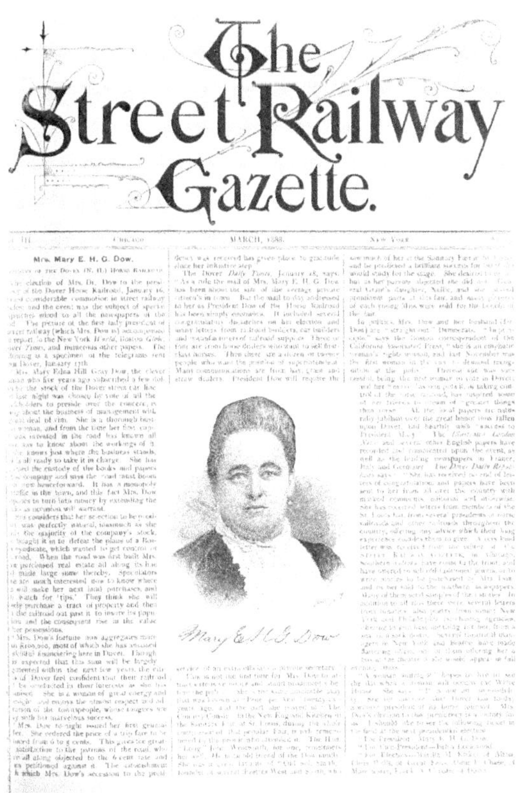

The Street Railway Gazette.

Chicago — MARCH, 1888. — New York

Mrs. Mary E. H. G. Dow.

Mary E. H. G. Dow

The March 1888 issue of the *Street Railway Gazette* featuring a full front-page story about Mary Dow. *Courtesy of the MIT Libraries.*

the stage with the daughter of Ulysses S. Grant. She was offered a chance to further her acting career but declined. Back in Dover, she served for a short time as an assistant principal at Rochester's high school. A committed suffragist, in 1887 she demanded and was given the right to vote—becoming the first woman in Dover to do so. Her elevation to the presidency of the DHR provided her with deep pride and confidence as to how far women could rise. When asked if she thought she would live to see a woman as president of the United States, she answered, "It is not an impossibility. See for instance that Dover has to-day a woman president of its horse railroad. [My] election to this presidency is a victory for us."

End of story? Not yet. Before she was married, Mary was a correspondent for several newspapers. At the New Hampshire State Fair, she took first prizes for best jams and canned fruits, best white and brown bread, best butter, best French Houdan and Buff Cochin chickens (both breeds were new to the United States at that time), best darning and best varieties of cakes and frosting. She was an exceptional gardener with the "finest asparagus bed in Dover." She was acknowledged to be a good shot with "gun, rifle and pistol," loved to hunt and fish and was an accomplished swimmer. She raised three children. And, as icing on the prize-winning cake, there was a large merchant vessel, the S/V *Mary E.H.G. Dow*, named for her. Perhaps Mary Dow should be the first woman on U.S. currency!

After Henry Burgett took control of the DHR, the railway was quickly electrified and renamed, and park construction began. On September 18, 1890, the park Burgett humbly named after himself opened for business. A circular distributed by his railway company described the park this way:

> *The air at the Park is of the purest and best. A good, cool breeze can be enjoyed there in the hottest of weather. The scenery around the lake is beautiful. A fleet of boats is there and a party can spend an hour pleasure rowing or sailing about the lake, or, if they do not care to row or sail, they can charter a steam launch at a very small expense and the trip around the lake is a most delightful one.*

Just to sweeten the pot, admission to the park was free if you rode the trolley to get there. In addition to the boats, the park's many features included a casino (in reality a large restaurant and dance hall); a pavilion (including a bowling alley); a 1,500-seat baseball stadium; a carousel, a 2,000-seat open-air theater featuring concerts, vaudeville reviews and plays; a bicycle racetrack; lawn tennis courts; swings; picnic tables; bear cage…bear cage?

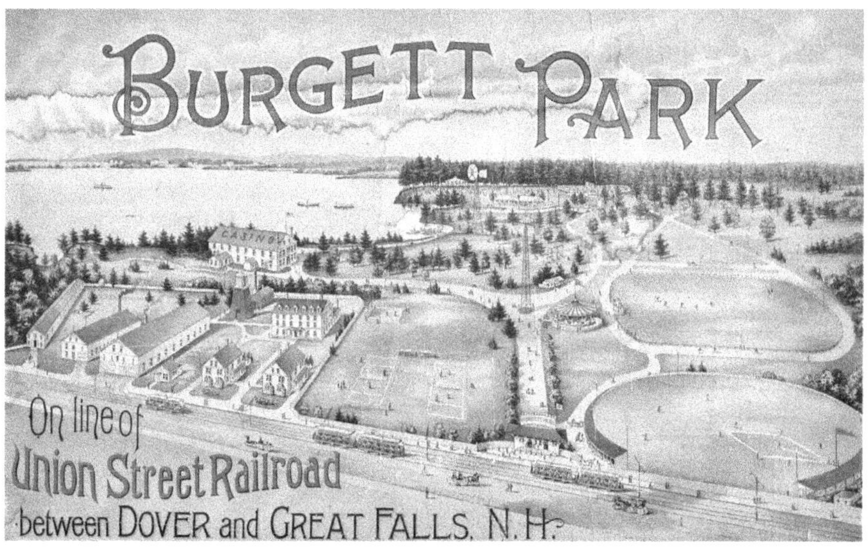

Original Burgett Park poster, circa 1890. *Courtesy of the Summersworth Historical Society.*

One has to wonder what made Burgett decide to throw a bear cage into an already wonderful amusement park. And the irony is that the bear cage is one of the few existing remainders of the park. Happily, by all accounts the bear cubs were well treated. Meanwhile, turn back to the Granite State Park chapter's 1953 aerial photo of the racetracks (page 100) and Willand Pond to see, on the edge of the photo to the right of the upper part of the pond, the still existing Central Park baseball field; the tree-lined park entrance just below, coming off High Street; and the trolley car barn in a rectangular clearing a bit farther down.

Burgett Park was renamed Central Park within a year of opening due to its central location relative to Dover, Rochester and Somersworth. When the trolley line went out of business in 1926, the fortunes of Central Park quickly declined. The casino was the last attraction, holding on until 1938, when Somersworth High held its junior prom there for the final time. After that, things kind of petered out. There are, however, a few notable related remnants still active today in the nearby area. The very name of Central Park lives on at an auto repair business on Somersworth's High Street across from the park's old entrance. On the same side of the street, just a few yards to the south, is a building dating from 1894 now in use as an office building but that at one time was the Central Park Inn. The original sign for the inn is proudly displayed at the Summersworth (Somersworth's original name) Historical Society. And very exciting to enlightened railroad enthusiasts everywhere is the fact that the 1890s trolley barn, where the railway's cars were stored and serviced and that is located across the street from the former inn, has been converted into New Hampshire's most unique state liquor store. Now there's synergy.

Although many folks have done things to help keep Central Park's memory alive, it took another Eagle Scout to come up with something special. For over twenty years, the cities of Dover and Somersworth have jointly maintained the Willand Pond area as a park with walking trails, outdoor exercise facilities and a fishing pond complete with boat ramp. But there had been no concerted effort to mark its history as an amusement park or preserve its few remaining remnants. In 2014, Somersworth resident David Brackett, of local Boy Scout Troop

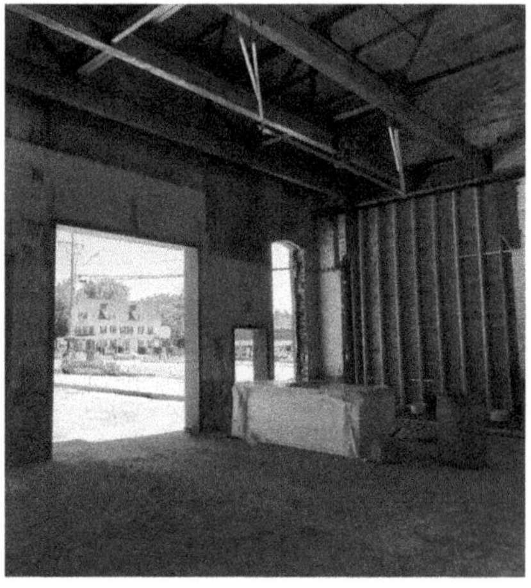

The building that once was the Central Park Inn as seen from inside the old streetcar barn during its renovation to become a New Hampshire Liquor & Wine Outlet. The former inn is now an office building. *Author's photo.*

This sign originally hung outside the Central Park Inn, which opened around 1894. The Central Park entrance was across the road. The sign now hangs in the Summersworth (Somersworth) Historical Society's museum. *Author's photo with permission of the museum.*

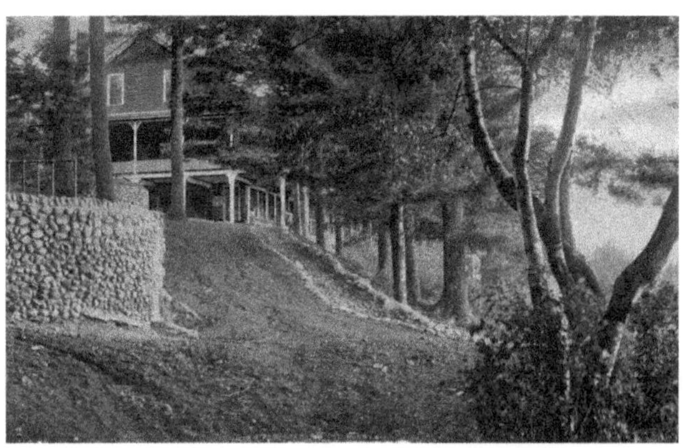

Early twentieth-century postcard showing (going up the hill on the left) the bear cage, the stone garden and the casino, which is long gone. *Courtesy of the Summersworth Historical Society.*

168 and an eighth grader at Portsmouth Christian Academy, came to the rescue and decided to make Central Park his Eagle project. Actually, he first visited the park's remains as a first grader and Tiger Cub Scout and realized way back then that this was to be his project. Like Henry Burgett 130 years earlier, David was inspired by the pond's quiet beauty, and he wanted to preserve its history.

Other than a few building foundation stones, there were very few other remnants from the park's heyday except for the run-down bear cage and a stone flower garden, which was much deteriorated and partially covered over with earth. Both of those can be seen in the vintage Central Park postcard image with the bear cage in front on the left, the stone garden beyond it up the hill and the Casino in the background. David organized over 100 people

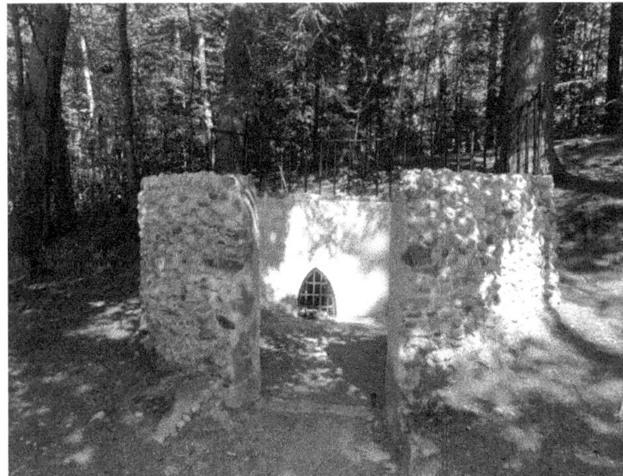

The restored Central Park bear cage. *Author's photo.*

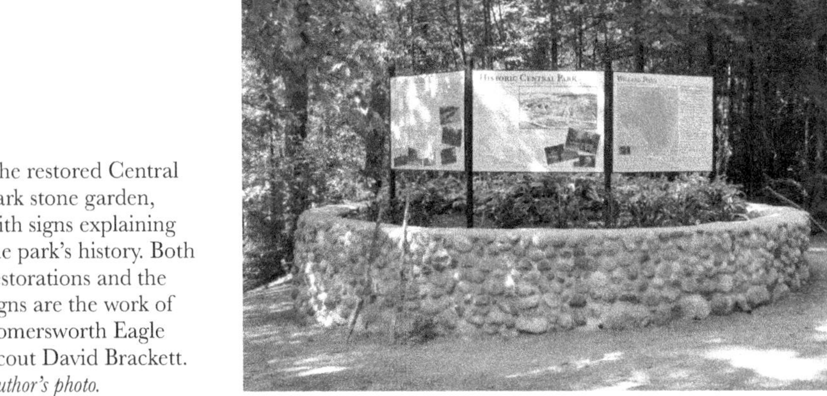

The restored Central Park stone garden, with signs explaining the park's history. Both restorations and the signs are the work of Somersworth Eagle Scout David Brackett. *Author's photo.*

to volunteer with labor and supplies, including many from local businesses. 1700 man-hours later the project was done. The accompanying photos show the outstanding results. The bear cage is beautifully renovated and the stone garden is completely restored. In the garden David placed several information boards chronicling the history of the park.

The remnants of Henry Burgett's beautiful park are still well worth a visit. Just yards away from busy roads, strip malls and neighborhoods, it is a delightful hidden oasis on the Dover/Somersworth border. If you visit, you will find joggers, people walking dogs and nature lovers in general enjoying the scenery while strolling along the pond's tranquil shores. The pond itself is the scene of folks fishing in the summer and ice skating in the winter. Bald eagles have been known to soar above the water. In addition to David's improvements, there is a children's playscape, as well as several fitness stations along the pond's path. A lovely picnic area on a small bluff overlooking the pond, complete with interpretive signs, was also an Eagle project, identified only with "K. Crawford, 2007" etched on the back of one of the signs. Benches at intervals along the path are the result of other Boy Scout projects. There are also some additional old Central Park remains to be seen, including the location of the hillside amphitheater, the occasional electrical wire crossbar high in the trees and the foundations of the casino veranda's pillars.

There are two entrances to the park. The Dover entrance is off Route 108/New Rochester Road, leading to the boat ramp. The other is easier to find. Just drive north from the Spaulding onto High Street/Route 9 in Somersworth, then hang a left at that wonderfully reimagined New Hampshire Liquor & Wine Outlet. Either way, the trip around the lake is still a most delightful one.

John Leighton, Age Nineteen, of Madbury

Regardless of his own ease, he strove to promote the present and everlasting good of those around him, and fell a victim to his unwearied and devoted attention to his sick relatives.
—unknown mourners

Initially, there were two sites that inspired this book. One was that small Henry Dearborn monument in Nottingham, and the other is just off Back River Road in Madbury. This road starts out with one name—Back River Road—as it heads south from Route 108 on the southwest side of Dover, becomes the Piscataqua Bridge Road for about a mile while passing through Madbury and then becomes Back River Road again as it enters Durham, a few thousand feet before it hits Route 4, where it ends. (Less than a mile west on Route 4 stands the Emery Farm, the oldest family farm in America, established in 1660.) At one time, the road connected to a bridge, built in 1794 and dismantled in 1855, across the Piscataqua River to Newington. The road exists because in the very earliest of days of settlement in Dover, it was part of the Post Road between Dover and Portsmouth. It is very lightly traveled because it's basically a short north–south connecter. These days, the nearby Spaulding Turnpike takes virtually all northbound or southbound through traffic.

In 1633, Thomas Leighton was granted ten acres of land (in what was then Dover) described in 1647 as "butting on the Back River west, and on John Damm's lott on the north, and on ye lane to the back Cove, on the

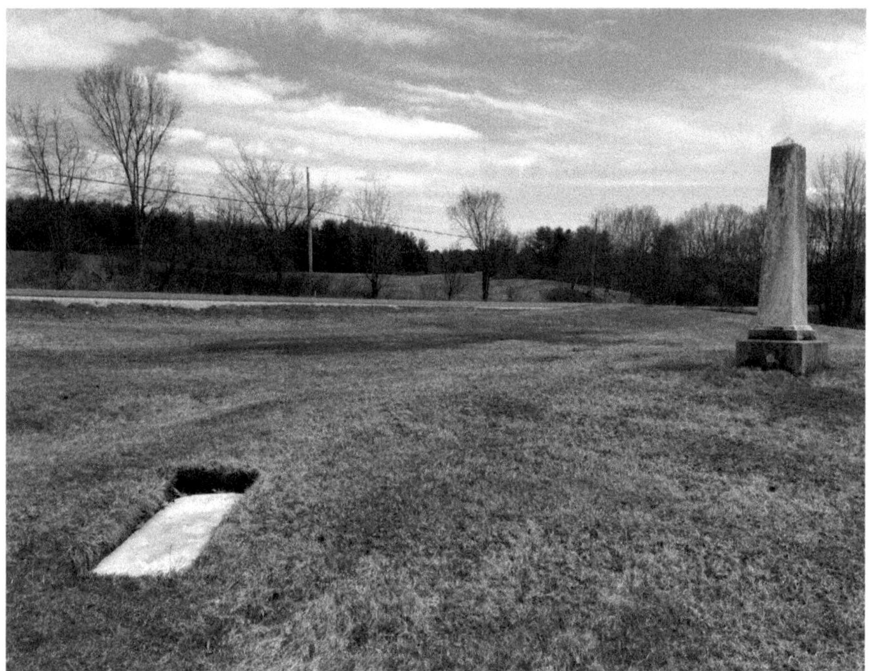

The peaceful grounds of the Leighton family memorials, Madbury. *Author's photo.*

south." Born in Great Britain (some biographies say England, others say Scotland) around 1604, Leighton was part of the group of Puritans led by Captain Thomas Wiggin, who brought all the religious angst described in the Dover Point meetinghouse chapter. Eventually, Leighton amassed hundreds of acres of land and became one of the wealthiest men in Dover. The area of his original grant was known for many years as Leighton Hill, and it is this place that Leighton family descendants, of whom there are thousands throughout the United States, view as their ancestral home.

Take that drive south down Back River Road from Dover and after a couple of miles you will come to the crest of Leighton Hill. There, you will be treated to a beautifully serene view across meadows and woods toward the Little Bay. It is especially pleasing in the spring when the fields are green but the leaves are not filled in, resulting in an open view to the water. That quiet road is also about the last place one would expect to see a fairly impressive monument in the middle of a pasture, visible down the hill to the right of the road. A neatly mowed pathway leads to a small mound upon which stands the Leighton Family Monument. A few feet away, there is a gravestone lying flat, several inches below ground level. Had you visited the site a few years ago, you would have found the gravestone covered by cloudy Plexiglas with a weather-stained sheet of paper attached underneath showing "LEIGHTON" as a heading. The upright monument on the site was erected in 1885, as requested by Mary Ann Leighton Rollins upon her death, in honor of her family and her Leighton ancestors who first settled these ten acres. The roughly six-foot obelisk reads:

In memory of the
Leighton household
erected by
Mrs. Mary A. Leighton
Rollins.
1885.

When the Leighton descendants sold the land, it was agreed that subsequent landowners would maintain the monument and grounds around it. If you visit the site, now in the town of Madbury—which split from Dover and was incorporated in 1775—you will see that the current landowner has done an excellent job of honoring that agreement. Mary Ann Leighton, born in 1800, was the eldest child of John and Abigail Leighton of Dover. She was married to John Anthony Rollins, with whom she had eight children. One of them, Hiram Rollins, became a U.S. Army brigadier general. Rollinsford, New Hampshire, was named after Hiram's ancestor Ichabod Rollins, an early Rollinsford settler who served in the Revolutionary Congress in Exeter. John Leighton, born in 1806, was the youngest of John and Abigail Leighton's four children, and it is his name on the gravestone. The sheet of paper was attached beneath the Plexiglas because that covering was too cloudy to see through to the ground. The inscription on the headstone reads:

> *This stone is erected in Memory of John Leighton by a number of his young friends from Salem, Mass. He was an ardent disciple of the Lord Jesus, His advantages were few his course short; but he has left behind a name which will be precious to many, regardless of his own ease he strove to promote the present and everlasting good of those around him, and fell a victim to his unwearied and devoted attention to his sick relatives, Nov. 2, 1825; AEt* [of age]. *19.*

The paper then goes on to refer to the work done in 2007 by members of the Leighton family, led by Nancy Leighton Auclair and her husband,

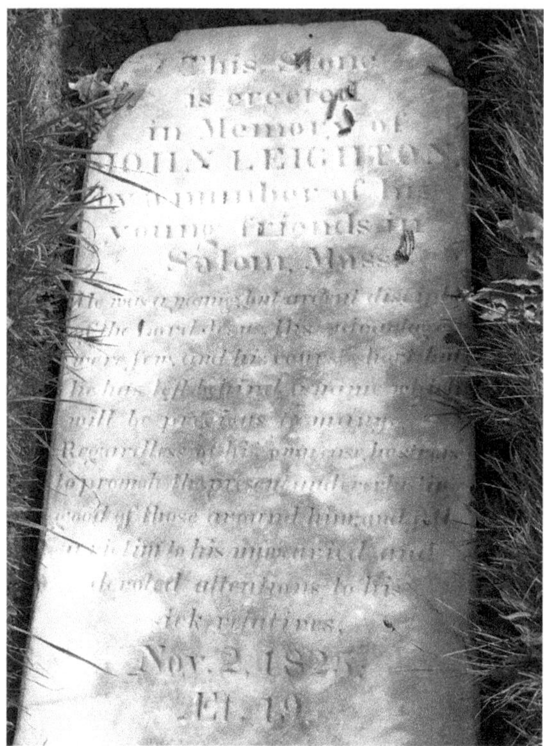

John Leighton's gravestone. *Author's photo.*

Raymond, in preserving and protecting the monuments at the site. At that time, they were living just over the border in Maine.

When asked about her work on the grave, Nancy said that when she and her family fixed up the Leighton family site, they felt that John's headstone was too fragile to put back upright, so they left it lying flat on the ground and put on the Plexiglas covering. Nancy mentioned that there are other burials on the site, perhaps six more. She went on to say that she had done a bit of looking into John's story when she improved the site but didn't find out much more than what was provided on his headstone. And, she added, she unfortunately didn't know of anyone who might have more knowledge of John. When the grass has been freshly cut, a few of the unmarked stones Nancy mentioned can definitely be easily seen. John's stone, however, is the only one with any kind of inscription on it. Clearly, some people cared deeply about him.

The whole scene is very touching: the pastoral setting; the thought of the modern-day Leightons caring for an old site, as did Mary Ann Leighton in 1885, sixty years after her brother's death; the current landholders' careful stewardship of the plot; John's young friends traveling from Salem to Dover (not an easy journey in 1825) for his funeral and providing the heartfelt memorial stone honoring him; and most of all, of course, the brief story of John Leighton himself—leaving his new home and friends in Salem to care for sick relatives and paying the ultimate price after he nursed them back to health. It turns out that many others are moved by John's story as well. An Internet search of "John Leighton—Dover, NH" turns up several sites regarding John, most of them referring to the inscription on his tombstone. A particularly good source is FindAGrave.com, a worldwide site logging millions of gravestones and the human stories behind them, John Leighton being one of them. There is also a Leighton family blog containing postings from people around the country trying to find out more about young John.

The common thread of all those who know of John is the desire to learn more of the story behind the young man who has engendered such strong feelings across the miles, the years and the generations. The Portsmouth Athenaeum, a wonderful private library on Market Square that has been around since 1817, is an outstanding resource for historical research, especially obscure items. Its excellent database contains two newspaper obituaries about John. One is a simple obituary in the November 12, 1825 issue of the *Portsmouth Journal of Literature and Politics* reading, "In Madbury, Mr. John Leighton, aged 19." The other, a November 8, 1825 issue of the *New Hampshire Republican*, a Dover newspaper, had a much more detailed listing:

> *In Madbury, near Piscataqua Bridge, Mr. John Leighton aged 19. In the death of this young man his family connexions have sustained a loss which is most deeply felt, and which is irreparable. He was a youth of modest merit, and of much promise. Within a short period he had become hopefully pious, and had united with the Tabernacle Church in Salem where he had recently lived. Since his return to his friends in this vicinity he has been unremitted in his attentions to them thro' a long course of most painful and distressing sickness. His religion was the religion of kindness and peace. After his relatives had recovered, he was seized with a violent fever, which, in a few days, terminated his short but useful life. He died in the faith of Jesus,—in the hopes and comforts of the Gospel.*

This incredibly moving obituary explained what happened to John but left many other questions still unanswered. Why did John leave the Dover area? Who were the sick relatives to whom he attended? Who were the grieving young friends who provided the memorial stone and made the effort to have it brought the sixty miles to Madbury? The other common thread among those Leighton kin from Maine to California who knew of John is that no one knows much more than what is on his gravestone.

Betsey Bennett is the historian of Salem's Tabernacle Church, which was founded in 1629. She says that even though the current Tabernacle Church is the third on this site (circa 1924), she believes that John would feel very at home inside today's church. The sanctuary of the current church does indeed have a feel very similar to the nineteenth-century building that John likely would have known. Betsey went on to say that in the early nineteenth century, Salem was a booming seaport and shipbuilding town, rivaling Boston and indeed the whole Northeast coast, with lots of jobs and excitement available. The Salem Tabernacle Church is Congregational. Each pillar on its front portico has a symbolic front door attached to it, and each of these doors is painted with a different color of the rainbow, symbolizing acceptance of all. Therefore, it might seem a bit surprising to learn that the Congregationalists, one of the most open and accepting of modern religions (they almost always display the rainbow flag out front), grew out of the Puritans, who are usually portrayed as being rigid and unforgiving. The fact is, despite quite an evolution in certain beliefs, the common thread in the faith has always been the idea of independent congregations free from the dogma and hierarchy of a central church, originally the Church of England.

Stone by Stone is a book by University of Connecticut professor Robert M. Thompson about the stone walls of New England. The book is about a lot more than "piles of rocks"; it also chronicles New England's early agricultural and economic history. Thompson explains that in 1819, a financial panic engulfed the United States, brought on by speculation and overextended credit, causing farm product prices to fall to half of their long-term average values. Then along came the Erie Canal and the railroads making cheaper farm products from more efficient farms in New York and beyond widely available to consumers in the East. Thus began the decline of agriculture in New England. That explains why there are so many stone walls running through the woods in New Hampshire. After nearly two hundred years, all that walled-off farmland has reverted to forest. So perhaps our John, now a proper young man starting out in life, figured prospects were a whole lot brighter in Salem than on the struggling farms of New Hampshire.

Meanwhile, in the records room at the Tabernacle Church there is a rather nondescript loose-leaf binder labeled "Membership lists 1745–1915." In it are photocopies of handwritten lists detailing folks joining—

and leaving—the church. One page in the book turned up a listing of John (bottom right, fourth from the bottom) as having joined the church in February 1825. It also looks like next to John's name, "dead" is written, perhaps in pencil, as the sad reason for his leaving the church. There is one more intriguing record: the admission to the church of a James Leighton in November 1824 (top left, fourth from the top), just three months before John was admitted. A later entry after his name shows that he "left town sick" sometime after his formal joining. Could he have been one of the sick relatives whom John went home to tend? Perhaps *The Leighton Genealogy*, an exhaustive collection published by Perley Leighton in 1989, could provide some clues. As it turned out, there were around a dozen "James Leightons" who could have been contemporaries of John (that is, born between 1790 through 1810, in the ballpark of John's birth in 1806). Due to factors such as infant mortality or the individual passing away before 1825 (the year John was tending to his sick relatives), there were only about four who could have been the James in the Tabernacle Church record. But there's no way of finally knowing, as there isn't any more information on those four Jameses available.

There are Leighton kin in the United States from Maine to California, including New Hampshire, Missouri, Maryland, Alabama and Connecticut, to name a few. Unfortunately, all of them contacted knew little or nothing of John, other than a few knowing about the information on the tombstone.

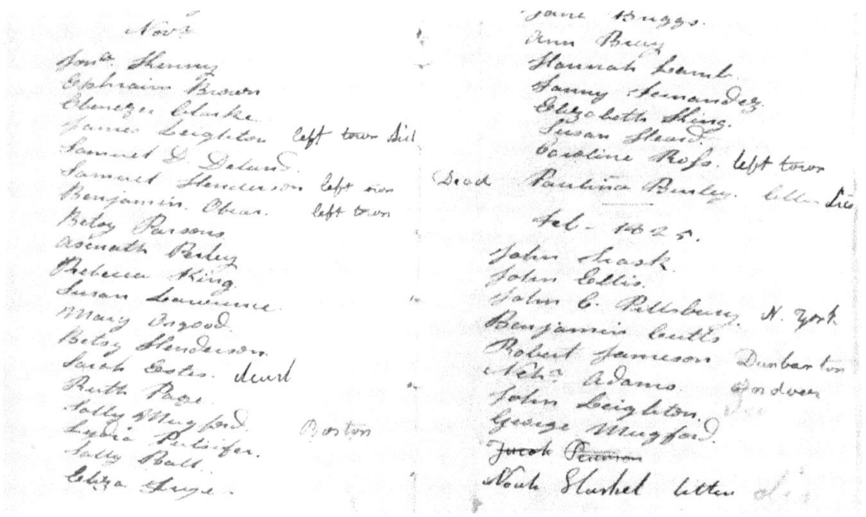

Nov.

Jon.a Henry
Ephraim Brown
Ebenezer Clarke
James Leighton left town sick
Samuel D. Deland
Samuel Henderson left town
Benjamin Obear. left town
Betsy Parsons
Asenath Pedley
Rebecca King
Susan Lawrence
Mary Osgood
Betsy Henderson
Sarah Estes. dead
Ruth Page
Sally Mugford
Lydia Pelsifer. Boston
Sally Ball
Eliza [illegible]

Jane Briggs.
Ann Berry
Hannah Lamb
Fanny Fernandez
Elizabeth King.
Susan Heard
Caroline Ross. left town
Dead Paulina Bailey. [illegible]

Feb. 1825.

John Trask.
John Ellis.
John C. Pillsbury N. York
Benjamin Cutts
Robert Jameson Dunbarton
Neh.a Adams. Andover
John Leighton.
George Mugford
~~Jacob Peirson~~
Noah Hashel letter

November 1824 and February 1825 Tabernacle Church of Salem membership lists. *Author's photo with permission of the Tabernacle Church.*

One thing was for sure, however: any Leighton family members who had heard about young John were anxious to find out more about his story. In a strange twist of fate, a reported "John Leighton—Dover" Internet search turned up a very surprising result: "1825 Printed Headstone Memorial to Mr. John Leighton of Dover, New Hampshire—eBay."

The seller's site indicated that he was from the San Francisco area. The gentleman selling it reported that he had bought it at a flea market in Sausalito in the 1980s and that he knew nothing else about it. Checking *The Leighton Genealogy*, one learns that another sister of John's, Ruth, born in 1802, moved to California in 1849 with her second husband, Jonathan Locke, to join the gold rush. Ruth died in Sausalito in 1885—the same year

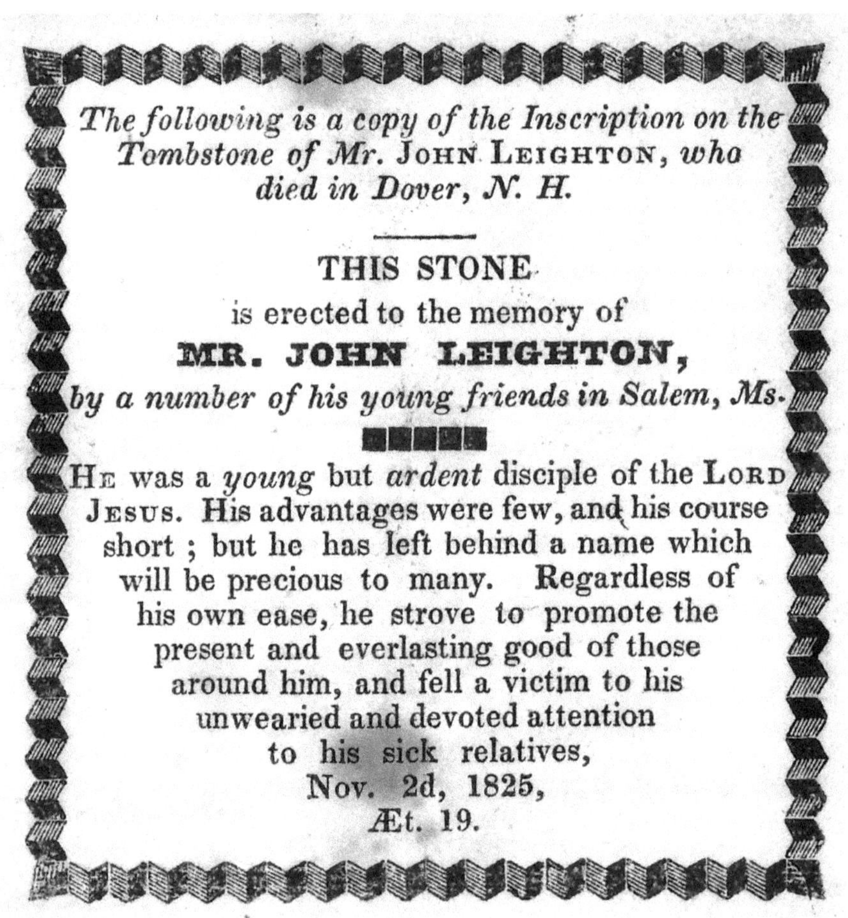

The following is a copy of the Inscription on the Tombstone of Mr. JOHN LEIGHTON, *who died in Dover, N. H.*

THIS STONE
is erected to the memory of
MR. JOHN LEIGHTON,
by a number of his young friends in Salem, Ms.

HE was a *young* but *ardent* disciple of the LORD JESUS. His advantages were few, and his course short ; but he has left behind a name which will be precious to many. Regardless of his own ease, he strove to promote the present and everlasting good of those around him, and fell a victim to his unwearied and devoted attention to his sick relatives,
Nov. 2d, 1825,
Æt. 19.

Ruth Leighton's memorial card for her brother, rescued from eBay and now back with the Leighton family. *Courtesy of Gayle Van Dyke.*

as her older sister Mary Anne, the one who had the monument erected. Obviously, a still grieving Ruth brought her brother's funeral memorial with her to California, where it was carefully tended for some 170 years, until it ended up fortuitously at that flea market. John's memorial card is now safely back in the hands of a member of the Leighton family.

That memorial card and the newspaper obituaries referenced Dover as the place of John's funeral. Since the Tabernacle Church of Salem was Congregational, it seemed very likely that the funeral took place at Dover's First Parish Church, also Congregational. Diane Fiske, the church historian, conducted an extensive search of church records, much of it looking through tedious microfiche files. Unfortunately, she found that the church had no funeral records going back as far as 1825.

One would surmise that John's funeral service was indeed through the Dover First Parish Church, even though records don't go back that far, because it's the most logical choice—but it isn't necessarily so. The James Leighton from the Salem Tabernacle who left town sick could very well be one of the relatives young John took care of, but maybe he wasn't. And there is no information at all on the grieving young friends who provided his heart-rending gravestone. As for those good friends, they could have been from his Salem church; they could have been work mates; they could have been in the same boardinghouse; or any combination of these. One thing's for sure: they were a tight bunch who sorely missed their friend. All that information may very well be out there somewhere, but ultimately, those facts don't really matter.

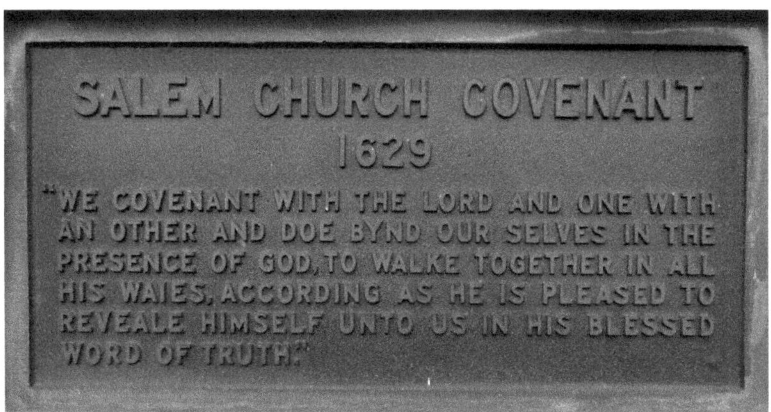

The Tabernacle Church covenant, located next to the church entrance. *Author's photo.*

The Tabernacle Church covenant reads in part: "We covenant with the Lord and one with an other...to walke together in all His waies [ways]." John Leighton, in his few short months as a member of the Salem Tabernacle Church, surely lived its covenant.

Of all the individuals brought to light in this book—Henry Dearborn, Mary Dow, Malvina Hoffman, Joseph Coe, to name a few—by far the least information is known about John Leighton. He was born in 1806, probably in Dover or Madbury; joined the Salem Tabernacle Church in February 1825; and by November of that same year had died of an illness that in all likelihood he contracted from the sick relatives he nursed back to health. Although this is by no means a happy story, it certainly is an inspiring one that deserves telling. When you reach the crest of Leighton's Hill while driving down Back River Road, pause a moment to take in the peaceful place where John has been laid to rest and contemplate these words from John's FindAGrave site, posted by "Gayle":

> *Not much is known about him except for the fact that to be 19 and to selflessly care for sick family members at the cost of your own safety...and then to have such extraordinary friends who would bring him the 60 miles from Salem to Dover and have a gravestone inscribed with such a heartfelt message speaks to what type of a young man he must have been.*

Bibliography

Dr. Dearborn, the DAR and Nottingham Square

Bancroft, George. *History of the United States.* Vol. 4. New York: D. Appleton, 1889.

Brown, Lloyd A., Howard Henry Peckham and Hermon Dunlop Smith. *Revolutionary War Journals of Henry Dearborn*. Chicago: Caxton Club, 1939.

Coffin, Charles. *The Lives and Services of Major General John Thomas, Colonel Thomas Knowlton, Colonel Alexander Scammell, Major General Henry Dearborn.* New York: Egbert, Hovey & King, 1845.

Cogswell, Elliot Colby. *History of Nottingham, Deerfield and Northfield, New Hampshire*. Manchester, NH: John B. Clarke, 1878.

Dearborn, Henry. *An Account of the Battle of Bunker Hill*. Boston: Munroe & Francis, 1818.

Encyclopedia.com. "Dearborn wagons." 2016.

Hale, Edward Everett. "Memories of a Hundred Years." *The Outlook* 70, no. 1 (January 4, 1902).

Jirka, Frank, MD. *American Doctors of Destiny*. Chicago: Normandie House, 1940.

McGee, W.E. *Men of Granite*. Portsmouth, NH: Peter E. Randell, Publisher, 2007.

Page, Edwin L. "Nottingham and Epsom Minute Men." Manuscript, 1955.

Vineyard, Ron. "Stage Waggons and Coaches." Colonial Williamsburg Foundation Library, August 2000.

LONDON BRIDGE, WINDHAM: NOT IN LONDON, NOT A BRIDGE

Garvin, Dr. James. "London Bridge Road Causeway." Determination of Eligibility, New Hampshire Division of Historical Resources, 2006.

Hurd, D.H. *Town & City Atlas of the State of New Hampshire*. Boston: D.H. Hurd Publishing Company, 1892.

Morrison, Leonard Allison. *Supplement to the History of Windham in New Hampshire*. Boston: Damrell and Upham, 1892.

Russell, Jenna. "1799 Bridge Divides N.H. Town." *Boston Globe*, March 6, 2006.

United States Census Bureau.

LITTLE BOAR'S HEAD

Boston Globe. "Hampton Beach 'Motif No. 1' (The Hampton Beach Fish Houses)." August 25, 1952 (Lane Memorial Library reprint).

Hampton Union. "Letters to the Editor on the Fish House Case." July 31, September 11, 2007 (Lane Memorial Library reprint).

———. "Malvina Hoffman Remembered." September 22, 1987 (Lane Memorial Library reprint).

Hobbs, Stillman M., and Helen D. Hobbs. *The Way It Was in North Hampton*. Seabrook, NH: Withy Press, 1978.

Living Places. "Little Boar's Head Historic District." Gombach Group, 2018.

Mausolf, Lisa B. "Little Boar's Head Historic District." National Register of Historic Places Registration Form, National Park Service, 1999.

Naval History Blog. "Remembering the USS Squalus 75 Years Later." U.S. Naval Institute, 2014.

New England Historical Society. "The Greatest Submarine Rescue Ever: Saving the Squalus." 2018.

New York Times. Malvina Hoffman obituary, July 11, 1961.

Parsons, Langdon. *History of the Town of Rye, New Hampshire*. Concord, NH: Rumford Printing Company, 1905.

Rogers, Stillman. *It Happened in New Hampshire*. Guilford, CT: Globe Pequot Press, 2004.

soapstonesculpture.com. "Malvina Hoffman—A Tribute."

Southworth, Robert A., and Katherine Southworth, et al. *First Report of the Historic District Commission of the Village District of Little Boar's Head*. July 1994.

Workers of the Federal Writers Project. *New Hampshire: A Guide to the Granite State*. Boston: Houghton Mifflin Company, 1938.

THE MEETINGHOUSE AT DOVER POINT

Bolton, Charles Knowles. *The Founders, Portraits of Persons Born Abroad Who Came to the North American Colonies before the Year 1701*. Boston: Boston Athenaeum, 1919–26.

Bryant, Donald. *History of the First Parish Church: Founded 1633, Dover, New Hampshire*. Dover, NH: Bryant, 2002.

Bryant, Donald, and David Starbuck. "First Parish Church—Dover Point Site." National Register of Historic Places Nomination, Inventory Form, National Park Service, 1983.

Quint, Alonzo. "The First Church in Dover, and Its Pastor." *Granite Monthly*, November 1877.

———. *The First Parish in Dover*. Dover, NH, 1884.

Quint, Alonzo, and John Scales. *Historical Memoranda Concerning Persons and Places in Old Dover, N.H.* Dover, NH: Dover Enquirer, 1900.

Scales, John. *Colonial Era History of Dover New Hampshire*. Manchester, NH: J.B. Clarke Company, 1923.

———. *History of Strafford County New Hampshire*. Chicago: Richmond-Arnold Publishing Company, 1914.

Seavey, Annie. "First Parish Church, 1638." Manuscript, circa 1935.

Speare, Eva A. *Stories of New Hampshire*. N.p.: New Hampshire Publishing Company, 1975.

Stackpole, Everett. *History of New Hampshire*. Vol. 1. New York: American Historical Society, 1916.

Wadleigh, George. *Notable Events in the History of Dover New Hampshire*. Dover, NH, 1882/1913.

Welch, Robert. "Old Dover—An Historical Sketch of Old Dover." Commemorative newspaper, 1875.

Whitehouse, Robert. "Dover, N.H. Churches." Manuscript, 1987.

BROTH HILL, CITY OF SETH

Coe, Joseph. *The True American.* Concord, NH: I.S. Boyd, 1840.

Hatfield, Mark. *Vice Presidents of the United States 1789–1993.* Washington, D.C.: U.S. Government Printing Office, 1997.

Hiatt, Bernard. "Durham Historic District." National Register of Historic Places Nomination, Inventory Form, National Park Service, 1980.

Living Places. "Durham Historic District." Gombach Group, 2011.

Stackpole, Everett, Lucien Thompson and Winthrop Meserve. *History of the Town of Durham* (1913). Republished, Somersworth: New Hampshire Press, 1973.

Thompson, Mary. *Landmarks in Ancient Dover, New Hampshire.* Concord, NH: Republican Press Association, 1892.

TOWN POUNDS: STRAYS, REEVES AND POUNDERS

atlasofnewengland.wordpress.com. "Town Pounds."

flickr.com. "Project: NH Town Pounds."

gatesheadhistory.com/pinfolds (UK). "Village Pounds."

geocaching.com. "Town Pounds."

MacRury, Elizabeth B. "New Hampshire's Town Pounds." *New Hampshire Profiles,* September 1974.

Nutting, Wallace. *New Hampshire Beautiful.* Framingham, MA: Old America Company, 1923.

stonestructures.org. "Town Pounds."

thefamilytapestry.blogspot.com (AUS). "Town Pounds."

Town Animal Pound Project. Manchester Junior Women's Club, 1975.

United States Census Bureau.

waymarking.com. "Town Pounds."

DOVER SPEEDWAY AT GRANITE STATE PARK

Brighton, Raymond. *Frank Jones King of the Ale Makers*. N.p.: Peter E. Randall Publisher, 1976.

Crocco, Charles. "The Roaring Stock." Manuscript, Dover, NH, 1959.

Manchester Union Leader, March 20, 2013.

Nashua Telegraph, May 28, 1947.

Nye, A.E.G. *Dover, New Hampshire Its History and Industries*. Foster's Daily Democrat Twenty-Fifth Anniversary Souvenir, 1898.

Scales, John. *History of Strafford County New Hampshire*. Chicago: Richmond-Arnold Publishing Company, 1914.

ATKINSON ACADEMY: AMERICA'S OLDEST

American Institute of Physics. "Oral History Interview with Ralph Alanson Sawyer." Parts 1 and 2. March 16, 1967, and September 24, 1970.

Atkinson Academy Catalogue. 1837, 1852, 1853, 1896, 1902.

Barnum, Louise Noyes. *Atkinson Then and Now*. N.p.: Atkinson Historical Society, 1975, 1999.

Bush, Dr. George Gary. *History of Education in New Hampshire*. Washington, D.C.: Government Printing Office, 1898.

Charlton, Edwin A. *New Hampshire As It Is*. Claremont, NH: Tracy and Company, 1856.

Cogswell, Dr. William. Atkinson Academy address, 1887.

Janik, Erika. "The Shape of Your Head and the Shape of Your Mind." TheAtlantic.com, January 6, 2014.

Marr, Harriet Webster. *Atkinson Academy: The Early Years*. N.p.: John E. Stewart Company, 1940.

Michigan Alumnus. "Symposium Honors Dean-Emeritus Sawyer." Vol. LXXII, no. 2 (October 1965).

The New England Historical and Genealogical Register. Vol. 48, Boston, 1894.

New York Times. Ralph Sawyer obituary. December 7, 1978.

Old-Time New England: The Bulletin of the Society for the Preservation of New England Antiquities. "Ebenezer Clifford, Architect and Inventor." Vol. 65, nos. 3–4 (Winter–Spring 1975).

"Phrenology: Pseudo-scientific Practice." Britannica.com.

NEW HAMPSHIRE'S CENTRAL PARK

Catalfo, Alfred, Jr. *The History of the Town of Somersworth, 1623–1973.* Somersworth: New Hampshire Printers, 1973.

Dover Heritage Walking Tour guides, 1986, 1987, 1997.

Knapp, William. *Somersworth, an Historical Sketch.* Somersworth, NH: Free Press Publishing Company, 1894.

Scales, John. *History of Strafford County New Hampshire.* Chicago: Richmond-Arnold Publishing Company, 1914.

Stevens, Lydia. *Dover Horse Railroad.* Dover, NH: Northam Colonists Historical Association, March 2, 1912.

Street Railway Gazette. "Mrs. Mary E.H.G. Dow." Vol. III, no. 3 (March 1888).

Whitehouse, Robert. "Early Dover History." Manuscript, 1987.

Whitehouse, Robert, and Tom Whitehouse. *Historic Rambles about Dover.* N.p.: Robert A. Whitehouse, 1990.

JOHN LEIGHTON, AGE NINETEEN, OF MADBURY

findagrave.com. "John Leighton—Dover."

geneaolgy.com. "John Leighton—Dover."

lahfamilytree.com. "John Leighton—Dover."

Leighton, Perley. *A Leighton Genealogy.* Boston: New England Historic Genealogical Society, 1989.

New Hampshire Republican. John Leighton obituary. Vol. 3, issue 43 (November 8, 1825).

Thompson, Robert M. *Stone by Stone.* New York: Walker and Company, 2002.

About the Author

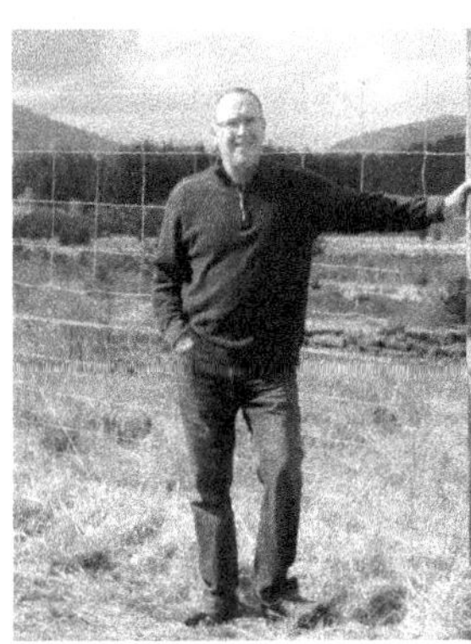

Terry Nelson was an educator for forty years. His last position before retiring was as an assistant principal for Southside Middle School in Manchester, the home of the Spartans. He and his wife, Barbara, live in Dover with their little dog, Ellie.

www.ingramcontent.com/pod-product-compliance
Lightning Source LLC
LaVergne TN
LVHW052338100826
845147LV00020B/1099